Research Needs for Human Factors

Committee on Human Factors
Commission on Behavioral and Social Sciences
  and Education
National Research Council

NATIONAL ACADEMY PRESS
Washington, D.C.   1983

NOTICE: The project that is the subject of this report was approved by the Governing Board of the National Research Council, whose members are drawn from the councils of the National Academy of Sciences, the National Academy of Engineering, and the Institute of Medicine. The members of the committee responsible for the report were chosen for their special competences and with regard for appropriate balance.

This report has been reviewed by a group other than the authors according to procedures approved by a Report Review Committee consisting of members of the National Academy of Sciences, the National Academy of Engineering, and the Institute of Medicine.

The National Research Council was established by the National Academy of Sciences in 1916 to associate the broad community of science and technology with the Academy's purposes of furthering knowledge and of advising the federal government. The Council operates in accordance with general policies determined by the Academy under the authority of its congressional charter of 1863, which establishes the Academy as a private, nonprofit, self-governing membership corporation. The Council has become the principal operating agency of both the National Academy of Sciences and the National Academy of Engineering in the conduct of their services to the government, the public, and the scientific and engineering communities. It is administered jointly by both Academies and the Institute of Medicine. The National Academy of Engineering and the Institute of Medicine were established in 1964 and 1970, respectively, under the charter of the National Academy of Sciences.

The Committee on Human Factors is sponsored jointly by the Air Force Office of Scientific Research, the Army Research Institute for the Behavioral and Social Sciences, the Office of Naval Research, and the National Aeronautics and Space Administration.

This work relates to the Department of the Navy contract N00014-81-C-0017 issued by the Office of Naval Research, and no official endorsement should be inferred.

The United States government has at least a royalty-free, nonexclusive and irrevocable license throughout the world for government purposes to publish, translate, reproduce, deliver, perform, dispose of, and to authorize others so to do, all or any portion of this work.

COMMITTEE ON HUMAN FACTORS

Richard W. Pew (Chair), Information Sciences Division,
    Bolt Beranek & Newman, Cambridge, Massachusetts
Nancy S. Anderson, Department of Psychology, University
    of Maryland
Alphonse Chapanis, Department of Psychology, Johns
    Hopkins University
Baruch Fischhoff, Decision Research, a branch of
    Perceptronics Inc., Eugene, Oregon
Irwin L. Goldstein, Department of Psychology, University
    of Maryland
K. H. Eberhard Kroemer, Industrial Engineering and
    Operations Research Department, Virginia Polytechnic
    Institute and State University
Herschel W. Leibowitz, Department of Psychology,
    Pennsylvania State University
J. C. R. Licklider, Department of Computer Science,
    Massachusetts Institute of Technology
Charles B. Perrow, Institution for Social and Policy
    Studies, Yale University
Michael Posner, Department of Psychology, University of
    Oregon (resigned April 1982)
Thomas B. Sheridan, Department of Mechanical Engineering,
    Massachusetts Institute of Technology
Jerome E. Singer, Department of Medical Psychology,
    Uniformed Services University of the Health Sciences
J. E. Keith Smith, Human Performance Center, University
    of Michigan (resigned October 1982)

Robert T. Hennessy, Study Director
Karen English, Administrative Secretary
Jeanne Richards, Administrative Secretary

PREFACE

The Committee on Human Factors was established in October 1980 under the joint sponsorship of the Office of Naval Research (ONR), the Air Force Office of Scientific Research (AFOSR), and the Army Research Institute for the Behavioral and Social Sciences (ARI) to identify basic research needs of the military services in support of human factors engineering applications and to make recommendations for basic research that will improve the foundations of this discipline. The committee's first meeting was held in December 1980; in October 1981 the National Aeronautics and Space Administration (NASA) joined the sponsors of the committee; and several other government agencies have expressed interest in the committee's work.

Human factors issues arise in every domain in which humans interact with the products of a technological society. Consequently, the knowledge brought to bear in human factors applications must be drawn from a wide range of scientific and engineering disciplines. Although no small group can be fully representative of all disciplines relevant to human factors, the expertise represented on the committee is quite broad. It includes specialists from the fields of engineering, biomechanics, psychology, cognitive science, and sociology as well as from human factors engineering. While other disciplines may be relevant, it is these that are expected to contribute most substantially to the basic data, theory, and methods needed to improve the scientific basis of human factors.

I wish to thank each member of the committee for their thoughtful contributions to this report. Individual members or small groups of members accepted primary responsibility for authoring each chapter. This authorship is acknowledged in the note at the beginning of each chapter. All committee members, whether they were authors or not, deliberated, reviewed, and contributed to improvements in the content of each chapter. I am especially grateful to them for their generous contribution of time, both in meetings and outside. Their efforts have contributed greatly to the quality of this report, which is truly a product of the full committee. Special thanks are due to the study director, Robert T. Hennessy, who contributed both technically and administratively to every step in the report's development. In addition, he has taken the kind of initiatives that made it possible for me to chair the committee with minimum effort and maximum reward.

Martin A. Tolcott and Gerald S. Malecki of the Office of Naval Research, Alfred R. Fregly of the Air Force Office of Scientific Research, Robert M. Sasmor of the Army Research Institute, and Melvin D. Montemerlo of the National Aeronautics and Space Administration, representatives of the committee's sponsors, have also made important contributions. Their support, encouragement, and identification of relevant issues have been most helpful.

I am grateful also to the participants in our workshop on applied methods: Stuart K. Card, David Meister, Donald L. Parks, Erich P. Prien, and John B. Shafer. Their broad understanding of applied methods and their cogent appraisal of the issues and needs in this area formed the basis for Chapter 7 of this report.

Several people were helpful to the committee in specific ways. At Wright-Patterson Air Force Base, Kenneth R. Boff organized a series of briefings by personnel from the Air Force Aerospace Medical Research Laboratory and the Air Force Human Resources Laboratory as well as tours of several of their research facilities. During the committee's visit to the Naval Training Equipment Center, Walter S. Chambers and Stanley C. Collyer arranged for presentations by members of the Human Factors Laboratory and briefed the committee on the research uses of the visual technology research simulator as well as demonstrating this device. I extend my appreciation to these individuals and organizations for their efforts on the committee's behalf.

Many other individuals also have contributed to the work of the committee and thereby to the contents of this report. A number of human factors professionals provided thoughtful and detailed responses to a survey on research issues. Others served as outside reviewers of particular chapters. Karen A. English and M. Jeanne Richards have served ably and conscientiously as administrative secretaries over the course of the committee's history. Christine L. McShane, editor for the Commission on Behavioral and Social Sciences and Education, through skill and perseverance greatly improved the style and clarity of this report. To all these individuals I express my sincere thanks for their significant contributions.

The committee's work is ongoing. This is the first in what is expected to be a continuing series of reports on issues in human factors research. I invite the reader's comments and reactions to this and future reports.

Richard W. Pew, Chair
Committee on Human Factors

CONTENTS

1 Introduction and Overview   1
2 Human Decision Making   12
3 Eliciting Expert Judgment   33
4 Supervisory Control Systems   49
5 User-Computer Interaction   78
6 Population Group Differences   125
7 Applied Methods   140

1

INTRODUCTION AND OVERVIEW

In the last several years the public has become sensitized to the importance of equipment designed to accommodate its human users. In the course of events at the Three Mile Island nuclear power plant many residents of Harrisburg were evacuated because of the accident precipitated by operators misinterpreting their instruments. Coal miners cover equipment lamps intended to illuminate the mine wall, because they object to the glare in their faces. The M-1, the most technologically sophisticated battle tank ever produced, is limited by the operating difficulties experienced by its crew. With computer terminals now pervasive in the workplace, more users are voicing their complaints about requirements to converse in arcane dialects of computer languages.

Each of these examples reflects a failure to consider the design of a system from the point of view of its potential users; thus it is not surprising that the public is demanding that more attention be paid to such considerations. These demands may be expressed in the decisions of jurors in court cases involving product liability, in the renewed emphasis on human factors in military and aeronautics laboratories, and in the increase in job opportunities for human factors professionals in the computer industry. In March 1982, over 1,000 people participated in a conference devoted to discussing how to make computers more user-oriented.

The historical roots of the human factors profession are in industrial engineering and in psychology. In the early 1900s Frederick W. Taylor coined the term <u>scientific management</u>, by which he meant the application of

---

The principal author of this chapter is Richard W. Pew.

scientific principles in the design of the industrial workplace. Although overzealous "Taylorism" resulted in some early mismanagement, his work formed one of the building blocks for modern industrial engineering and operations research.

During the latter stages of World War II, psychologists, who had been involved in the selection and training of aircraft pilots, were called on to take a novel perspective. Instead of selecting pilots to meet the severe demands of the cockpit, they were asked to select the cockpit design best suited to the characteristics of pilots. This approach reduced accidents and allowed a larger population of potential pilots to be certified. Because flying pushes the human body to its physiological limits, the effects of physiological stress on performance became a further consideration. After the war a small group of universities began training human factors specialists for research and development in the military services and the aerospace industry.

In 1957 the Human Factors Society was formed with 90 founding members; by 1977 the membership had grown to 1,956; and in the last five years the organization has expanded by an additional 50 percent. In addition, various engineering societies have formed groups related to human factors. The formation of this committee within the National Research Council in 1980 is the latest explicit recognition of the importance of human factors in today's technological society.

Human factors engineering can be defined as the application of scientific principles, methods, and data drawn from a variety of disciplines to the development of engineering systems in which people play a significant role. Successful application is measured by improved productivity, efficiency, safety, and acceptance of the resultant system design. The disciplines that may be applied to a particular problem include psychology, cognitive science, physiology, biomechanics, applied physical anthropology, and industrial and systems engineering. The systems range from the use of a simple tool by a consumer to multiperson sociotechnical systems. They typically include both technological and human components.

Human factors specialists from these and other disciplines are united by a singular perspective on the system design process: that design begins with an understanding of the user's role in overall system performance and that systems exist to serve their users, whether they are consumers, system operators, production workers, or maintenance crews. This user-oriented design philosophy acknowledges human variability as a design parameter. The resultant designs incorporate features that take advantage of unique human capabilities as well as build in safeguards to avoid or reduce the impact of unpredictable human error.

On the international scene this collection of activities has been called ergonomics, meaning the study of work. Its practitioners have placed somewhat more emphasis on biomechanics and the physiological costs of doing work than have human factors practitioners in the United States. Aside from this distinction, the two terms refer to the same collection of specialties.

While its foundations rest ultimately in the parent disciplines, human factors research focuses on the solution of system design problems involving more than one of these disciplines. Since World War II the major sources of funding for basic research underlying human factors work have been the National Aeronautics and Space Administration (NASA) and the military services. Since the passage of the Mansfield Amendment (Public Law 91-441, 1970) to the U.S. defense budget, which mandated a shift toward system development and away from basic research, the real dollar volume of research has not increased very much. What research there is has focused increasingly on short-term goals. As a result the basic knowledge needed to provide the underpinnings for human factors applications to new technology has not been generated. The need to reverse this trend is at least part of the reason that the military services and NASA have taken the initiative in sponsoring the work of this committee. This report reflects the committee's recommendations for needed research in terms of both long-term and short-term objectives.

This report does not attempt to cover the full scope of human factors engineering, even in relation to military and NASA needs. As the committee began discussing research needs, a wide range of possible topics was considered. Two of our meetings included tours and discussions of ongoing research in military laboratories. Committee members were encouraged to develop brief position papers on highlighted topics that were germane to their interests. The human factors community was surveyed through an article in the Bulletin of the Human Factors Society, and 116 responses were received; the survey results confirmed the importance of many of the topics already identified by the committee. Some topics were dropped, and some new papers were generated. Others were combined into coherent units; still others were deferred for further study or initiative.

The material in this report is the result of that process. Each chapter is designed to be a self-contained report of an important area in which research is needed. All the topics discussed here meet the following criteria: (1) each topic is germane to our military and NASA sponsors; (2) the topics are within the expertise of the committee; (3) each topic has been, in the opinion of the committee, incompletely addressed by previous or current military and civilian research efforts; and (4) the potential results of the recommended research will be important contributions to the scientific basis and practice of human factors. And the work of the committee is ongoing. In addition to the research areas presented in this report, work on a number of topics is in various stages of development: (1) organizational context in relation to design; (2) team performance; (3) simulation; (4) human performance modeling; (5) multicolor displays; (6) human factors education, and (7) accident reporting systems. We expect to address many of these as well as other topics in subsequent reports.

In the paragraphs that follow, the areas of research suggested by the committee are summarized together with some of our major recommendations. The chapters themselves provide a detailed elaboration of these topics.

HUMAN DECISION MAKING

A central issue in the understanding of human performance is human decision making. It has become even more important with the increased role of automation in complex modern systems ranging from military command, control, and communication systems to aircraft and process control systems. There has been much support for research on decision making over the last 15 years, particularly by the Defense Advanced Research Projects Agency and the Office for Naval Research. This research has tended to focus on formal decision theoretic constructions, which, while analytically powerful, have proved to be insufficiently robust to reflect the strengths and weaknesses of human decision-making capabilities. The committee recommends further research, with an emphasis on moving into uncharted areas.

Surprisingly, despite the effort devoted to decision-making research in general, there is still a need for research on how to structure practical decision problems and on improving the realism of models that claim to relate to decision-making performance. We do not know how to represent decision situations that evolve dynamically, nor do we have a systematic framework from which to consider decision aiding.

Furthermore, we are coming to realize that many planning activities actually involve decision making that cannot be modeled by enumerating the possible states of the world and courses of action in a unitary decision matrix. They often evolve over time in bits and pieces with limited central direction. We need a deeper understanding of such diffuse decision processes in order to provide effective computer aids for this kind of decision.

While previous work has led to many decision-making aids and models, no criteria or methodologies have been suggested for evaluating their relative merits. Until such comparisons are made, practitioners will continue to advocate their own products without a basis for choice among them. Finally, there is a persistent need for development of innovative ways of soliciting preference and relative value judgments from people, a problem that leads us directly to the second topic.

ELICITING EXPERT JUDGMENT

The application of expert judgment covers everything from medical evaluations to accident investigations. Although the subject matter ranges widely, it is our belief that there are generic, substantive research issues that should be addressed in a coherent program. These problems recur in diverse contexts for which elicitation methods either do not exist or are inadequately standardized across applications to yield consistent results. The research issues include (1) creating a common frame of reference from which to assess judgments among a group of experts; (2) formulating questions for experts in a way that is compatible with their mental structures or cognitive representations of a problem; (3) eliciting judgments about the quality of information; (4) detecting and identifying reporting bias in judgments; and (5) minimizing the effects of memory loss and distortion on the reporting of past events.

SUPERVISORY CONTROL SYSTEMS

Supervisory control is a relatively new conceptualization of system function that is playing an increasingly important role in automated systems. In such systems, operators supervise the semiautomatic control of a dynamic process, such as a chemical plant or railway system. Typically the operators work in teams and control computers, which in turn mediate information flow among various automatic components. Other examples of supervisory control systems are modern aircraft, medical intensive care units, power plants, and distributed command and control systems such as may be found in military operations or in manufacturing by robots. Such systems deemphasize the importance of human sensory and motor capabilities and emphasize complex perceptual and cognitive skills. This perspective is relatively new to practicing system designers; work is beginning to be sponsored in these areas, but much further development is needed.

Supervisory control may be thought of as a generalization from earlier work on monitoring and controlling complex systems; in that sense the foundations for modeling and theory are established. The theory must be greatly elaborated and extended, however, to meet the analysis requirements of current and future systems. As the human skills of thinking, reasoning, planning, and decision making become key, the models must be able to accommodate these human capacities and limitations. This is a choice opportunity to bring together work on control theory models and cognitive science representations.

Cognitive psychology is also advancing our understanding of the way in which resources are shared among various processes within the brain. This work has unexplored implications for understanding how to modify system design to change perceived workload, particularly in the complex tasks typical of supervisory control. Each of the military services has research programs focused on human workload analysis. In our opinion many of them are too application-oriented; they need a stronger focus on research to advance the knowledge base from which new application techniques will emerge.

Another key concern in supervisory control is prediction and the control of human error. Our understanding of this topic is in its infancy. We have no general theory of human error, although theories abound for human response time. Human reliability analysis has been in vogue for several years, but, as currently practiced, it simply uses the numerical aggregation of historical data on recorded human failure rates. It is weakest in just the situations in which it is most needed--when the activity involves complex diagnosis, situation assessment, and interaction with computers.

At the level of design, there are three major questions: how to design supervisory control tasks to accommodate human capabilities and limitations; how to organize and display the information needed to carry out these tasks; and how much control to delegate to the human versus the automatic parts of the system.

USER-COMPUTER INTERACTION

Since computers are already playing a major role in most new system developments, including supervisory control systems, issues of facilitating the learning and use by both computer professionals and novices has been accorded a chapter of its own.

At a March 1982 conference on user-computer interaction, more than 100 papers addressed a variety of topics related to hardware and software design. More than half of the 1,000 participants were system design specialists from industry and government. The committee believes that this level of interest foretells a heavy demand for scientific knowledge that has yet to be created. Although a number of industrial laboratories are supporting proprietary work, there is only one major funded collaborative effort between computer science and human factors specialists, that at Virginia Polytechnic Institute and State University (funded by the Office for Naval Research).

Most human factors research has been done in the area of computer hardware. Information is available on which to base design decisions concerning information display hardware and keyboards. Many alternative input devices, such as joy sticks, track balls, and light pens, have been studied in the context of specific applications. There is a need for further work on input devices that focuses on comparison among the full range of devices across a broad set of uses, including instruction, text processing, and graphics.

Automatic speech recognition and production have attracted much interest as the technology improves. Speech as an alternative to manual and visual modes of input and output needs systematic investigation. Fundamental work is necessary on the design of interactive speech dialogs that involve inherently sequential communication and potentially heavy memory demands on the listener.

As computer terminals are becoming pervasive in the white-collar workplace, concern is growing about the adverse effects on people from long-term use of terminals with cathode ray tubes (CRTs). A recent study by the National Institute for Occupational Safety and Health found no radiation hazards from CRTs but did find a substantial increase in worker complaints of fatigue and other health problems from sustained daily use. This study was not able to distinguish CRT design-based complaints from those relating to the task or other features of the workplace--and this is an urgent research need. In Europe, governments are now mandating standards for workplace designs. It will not be long before similar actions are taken in the United States and the research must begin now to anticipate them.

In the area of software design, research needs are only beginning to be filled. Effective design of sophisticated software implies understanding of human knowledge sytems and the ability to represent not only what a user knows but also how a user makes inferences from that information. There is a need for models of users' understanding of the system with which they are interacting, a problem that is important for supervisory control applications as well.

Perhaps the most neglected research area in computer system development is how to produce effective materials and reference information. While design principles developed for printed materials are useful for computer system documentation, there are documentation opportunities unique to interactive systems that we do not yet understand how to exploit effectively.

Finally, there is a need to understand in more detail the characteristics of the user population that make a difference in computer system design. We need research that suggests, in parametric terms, how changes in user characteristics should be reflected in system design changes.

The committee regards user-computer interaction as one of the most urgent topics on which to undertake research initiatives.

POPULATION GROUP DIFFERENCES

Through public sentiment as well as government legislation, our society has mandated the elimination of discrimination among population groups in the design of jobs and workplaces. In addition to racial discrimination, there is growing concern about discrimination on the basis of sex, age, and disability. We lack the research necessary to describe the nature and extent of performance differences among the various population groups about which discrimination is a concern. The committee believes it is in the national interest to undertake the research necessary to accommodate this relationship between population group differences and design.

It is not enough to consider population group differences per se. In some cases the effect of a group characteristic such as age on performance may depend on the value of some other variables, such as amount of training or level of interpersonal skills. It may be misleading to discover simply that performance deteriorates with age, when in fact training or experience may reverse that trend. Such interactions remain largely unexplored.

There is also a need to understand the way in which these differences in performance should influence workplace design or training procedures. We know how to write equipment specifications designed to fit 95 percent of a particular user population insofar as body dimensions are concerned, but for most other human performance characteristics we lack this knowledge.

APPLIED METHODS

Much human factors work is performed under constraints of money, time, and opportunity that preclude the use of the kind of experimental methods used in laboratory research. From necessity, human factors practitioners have adopted or developed a variety of applied methods for acquiring or organizing information related to human characteristics that arise in the context of system design, development, and evaluation. Examples of these methods are task analysis, information flow analysis, collection and analysis of survey data, evaluation of physical mock-ups, and the structured walk through. In contrast to the methods of scientific research, which are maintained and disseminated in university curricula and textbooks, and by specialists who devote careers to improving and inventing experimental design procedures, applied methods in human factors work are described only briefly in technical project reports, which are difficult to access, and efforts to improve or invent methods occur largely in connection with a particular project.

There is a clear need to develop a compendium of standard descriptions of the most important applied methods. This compendium would be valuable for use in human factors curricula in colleges and universities and for continuing education tutorials for human factors practitioners. Currently most knowledge of applied methods is gained through on-the-job experience.

Documenting existing applied methods, however, will not fulfill the methodological needs for all current and future system design purposes. Advances in computer technology applied to automation and supervisory control systems and computer systems themselves all have profound methodological implications for the analysis and description of the roles people play in these sytems. Existing methods such as workload analysis, protocol analysis, and function allocation require research to modify and extend their use in new applications in which the emphasis is on cognitive functions of operators rather than on the perceptual-motor functions prominent in old systems.

Similarly, there is a need to develop new methods to provide information of the type and form necessary to resolve such issues as translating task requirements into personnel selection criteria, deriving training requirements from functional requirements, and describing or evaluating the effects of task or system functions on the affective responses of personnel.

All the basic research needs addressed in this report require experimental investigations to provide the theory, principles, and data to support human factors work in the design and evaluation of systems. The application of the knowledge derived from basic research, however, will occur largely through the use of applied methods. Documentation of existing methods and research to extend and initiate methods to meet future needs are as essential as the substantive research to improve both the scientific basis and the practical effectiveness of human factors work.

CONCLUSION

System design and the world of work are undergoing profound changes. In a period when automation is replacing the need for finely tuned perceptual-motor activities by skilled operators, human productivity is no longer easily assessed in terms of unit output. New systems place increased demands on the cognitive and decision-making aspects of human performance. The role of people in systems is shifting to those of monitoring and directing otherwise automatic processes in industrial production, transportation, military operations, and office work.

These changes in human-machine relations both offer new opportunities and present new problems for system design. It is therefore timely and appropriate that the committee's first report of research needs in human factors emphasizes the importance of understanding fundamental cognitive processes and their role in interactive and supervisory control systems.

HUMAN DECISION MAKING

Work organizations, and those who staff them, rise and fall by their ability to make decisions. These may be major strategic decisions, such as the deployment of forces or inventories, or local tactical decisions, such as how to promote, motivate, and understand particular subordinates. To list the kinds of decisions that need to be made and the stakes that sometimes ride on them would be to repeat the obvious. Decisions are made explicitly whenever one consciously combines beliefs and values in order to choose a course of action. They are made implicitly whenever one relies on a ritualized response (habit, tradition) to cope with a choice between options. Repetition of past decisions may result in suboptimal choices; however, it may also provide a ready escape from the difficulties and expense of explicit decision making. The reasons decision making often seems (and is) so difficult are quite varied, as are the opportunities for interventions and the needs for human factors research to buttress those interventions.

One problem is information overload: More things need to be considered than can be held and manipulated in one's head simultaneously. Coping with such computational problems is an ideal task for computers, and there are a variety of software packages available that in one way or another combine decision makers' beliefs and values in order to produce a recommendation. Choosing between and using these decision aids forces one to face a second inherent difficulty of decision making: not knowing how to define (or structure) the decision problem and to assess one's own values, that is, how to make trade-offs

---

The principal author of this chapter is Baruch Fischhoff.

between competing objectives. Because analytic decision-making methods cannot operate without guidance on these issues, judgment is an inevitable part of the decision-making process, as is the need for judgment elicitation methods to complement the decision aid (see Chapter 3). A third difficulty is knowing when to stop analyzing and start acting. Taking that step requires one to assess the quality of the decision-making process and reconcile any remaining conflicts between the recommendation it produces and that produced by one's own intuitions. To help one through this step, a decision aid must reveal its own limits in ways that are psychologically meaningful. A fourth difficulty is that in many interesting decisions one knows too little to act confidently. When uncertainty is a fact of life, the role of good design is to ensure that the best use is made of all that is known.

The existence of these four problems is common knowledge. Their resolution is complicated by a fifth difficulty whose identification requires research: People's commonsense judgments are subject to robust-and systematic biases. These biases make it difficult to rely on intuition as a criterion for the adequacy of decisions and the methods that produce them. Decision aids must accommodate these biases and may require supplementary training exercises lest their recommendations be adopted only when they affirm intuitions that are known to be faulty.

Given the multitude of decisions that are made, any research or design effort that made even a minute contribution to the quality of a minute proportion of all decisions would bear a large benefit in absolute terms. Proving that such a benefit had been derived would be as difficult as it is in most areas of human factors work. Whenever uncertainty is involved, better decisions will produce outcomes only over the long run. That makes it difficult to establish the validity of bona fide improvements and easy to fall prey to highly touted methods with good face validity, but little else. A sound research base is needed not only to develop better decision-making methods, but also to give users a fighting chance at being able to identify which methods are indeed better for their purposes.

BACKGROUND

Ad hoc advice to decision makers can be traced from antiquity to the Sunday supplements. Scientific study of decision making probably begins with the development of statistical or Bayesian decision theory by Borel, Ramsey, de Finetti, von Neumann, Morgenstern, Venn, Wald, and others. They showed how to characterize and interrelate the primitives of a general model of decision-making situations, highlighting its subjective elements. The development of scientific decision aids could be traced in the work of Edwards, Raiffa, Schlaifer, and others, who showed how complex real-world decision situations could be interpreted in terms of the general model. Essential to this model is the notion that decision-making problems can be decomposed into components that can be assessed individually, then combined into a general recommendation that reflects the decision makers' best interest. Those components are typically described as options, beliefs, and values or alternatives, opinions, and preferences, or some equivalent triplet of terms. They are interrelated by an integration scheme called a decision rule or problem structure (e.g., Fischhoff, et al., 1981; Sage, 1981).

More generally, decision-making models typically envision four interrelated steps.

1. Identify all relevant courses of action among which the decision maker may choose. This choice among options (or alternatives) constitutes the act of decision; the deliberations that precede it are considered to be part of the decision-making process.

2. Identify the consequences (advantages) that may arise as a result of choosing each option; assess their relative attractiveness. In this act the decision maker's values find their expression. Although these values are essentially personal, they may be clarified by techniques such as multiattribute utility analysis and informed by economic techniques that attempt to establish the market value of consequences.

3. Assess the likelihood of these consequences' being realized. These probabilities may be elicited by straightforward judgmental methods or with the aid of more sophisticated techniques, such as fault tree and event tree analysis. If the decision maker knows exactly what will happen given each course of action, it then becomes a case of decision making under conditions of certainty and this stage drops out.

4. Integrate all these considerations in order to identify what appears to be the best option. Making the best of what is or could be known at the time of the

decision is the hallmark of good decision making. The decision maker is not to be held responsible if this action meets with misfortune and an undesired option is obtained.

These steps are both demanding and vague. Fulfilling them requires considerable attention to detail and may be accomplished in a variety of ways. Moreover, they may not even be followed sequentially, if insights gained at one step lead the decision maker to revise the analysis performed at a different step. This flexibility has produced a variety of models and methods of decision making whose interrelations are not always clearly specified.

The opportunity for routinizing and merchandising these decision-making procedures led to one of the academic and consulting growth industries of the 1970s. A wide variety of software packages and firms can now bring the fruits of these theoretical advances to practicing decision makers. Decision analysis, the most common name for these procedures, is part of the curriculum of most business schools. Although it has met considerable initial resistance from decision makers because of its novelty and because of the explicitness about values and beliefs that it requires, decision analysis seems to be gaining considerable acceptance (e.g., Bonczek, et al., 1981; Brown, et al., 1974; Raiffa, 1968). This acceptance seems, even now, to go beyond what could be justified on the basis of any empirical evidence of its efficacy. Figure 2-1 gives some examples of the contexts within which decision-aiding schemes relying on interactive computer systems have been operating and have been reported in the professional literature. Figure 2-2 is similar to the summary printout of one such scheme, which offers physicians on-line diagnoses of the causes of dyspepsia.

Behavioral decision theory (e.g., Einhorn and Hogarth, 1981; Slovic, et al., 1979; Wallsten, 1980) has taken decision aiding out of the realm of mathematics and merchandising into the realm of behavioral research by recognizing the role of judgment in structuring problems and in eliciting their components. Researchers in this field have studied, in varying degrees of detail, the psychological processes underlying these judgments and the ways in which they can be improved through training, task restructuring, and decision-aid design. A particular focus has been on the identification and eradication of judgmental biases. The research described below is that which seems to be needed to help behavioral decision research fulfill this role.

> Accounting--helping to assess the financial viability of
>   corporations.
> Clinical diagnosis--helping physicians to decide whether
>   to perform diagnostic procedures and how to
>   interpret their results.
> Counseling--helping people to choose careers or consider
>   having children.
> Energy--choosing where to site energy-producing
>   facilities.
> Meteorology--derivation of precipitation forecasts.
> Military--deciding whether troops are in an adequate
>   state of readiness; preplanning responses.
> Petroleum geology--allocation of resources for oil
>   exploration.
> Pharmaceutics--helping in monitoring field reports in
>   order to decide whether drugs need to be recalled.
> Research and development--deciding how to allocate funds.

FIGURE 2-1 Examples of Operating Decision-Aiding Systems

An important development in this research over the last decade has been its liberation from the mechanistic models of behavior inherited from economics and philosophy. The result has been more process-oriented theories, attempting to capture how people do make and would like to make decisions (e.g., Svenson, 1979). This change was prompted in part by the realization that mechanistic models offer little insight into central questions of applications, such as how action options are generated and when people are satisfied with the quality of their decisions. These developments are reflected in the research described below.

There may seem to be a natural enmity between those purveying techniques of decision analysis and those studying their behavioral underpinnings, with the latter revealing the limits of the procedures that the former are trying to sell. In general, however, there has been rather good cooperation between the two camps. Basic researchers have often chosen to study the problems that practitioners find most troublesome, and practitioners have often adopted basic researchers' suggestions for how to improve their craft. For example, in both commercial and government use, one can find software packages and decision-making procedures that have been redesigned in

ROTHERMAN AREA HEALTH AUTHORITY
   MONTAGU HOSPITAL
SYMPTOM PROCESSING PROJECT

UNIT NO. 1 456/89
SURNAME: Smith
FIRST NAMES: John

HISTORY SHEET

CLINICIAN: Dr. Gardner

SYMPTOMS INPUT TO COMPUTER

Male	Relief antacids
Age 60-69	Nightpain pres.
Site epigastric	Nausea present
Radiation none	Vomiting present
Duration 7m-1yr	Meals: pain immed
Pattern episodic	Haematemesis abs
Pain is moderate	No indigestion
Progress worse	Bowels OK
Aggd by food	Micturition OK

COMPUTER PROBABILITIES BASED ON THESE SYMPTOMS

```
                        0       25      50      75      100
FUNCTIONAL      22     ---------X-------------------------------
CHOLECYSTITIS    0     X----------------------------------------
DUODENAL ULCER   2     X----------------------------------------
GASTRIC ULCER   76     ---------------------------------X-------
CA. STOMACH      0     X----------------------------------------
none of these          -----------------------------------------
```

If you judge any of the above probabilities to be in error please adjust them accordingly.

PROVISIONAL DIAGNOSIS if appropriate is--_____

Level of confidence in this diagnosis.

```
     very tentative                      certain
         1         2         3         4         5
```

The highest probability has been assigned to GASTRIC ULCER. If this or any other probability is not in accordance with your own judgment, please indicate reasons for your conclusions.

FIGURE 2-2 Summary Printout of a Medical Decision-Aiding Scheme

Source: D. C. Barber and J. Fox (1981).

response to basic research. Established channels (e.g., conferences, paper distribution lists) exist for members of this community to communicate with one another. Many of the leading practitioners have doctoral-level training, usually in psychology, management science, operations research, or systems engineering, and maintain academic contacts. Indeed, the quantity of basic research has been reduced by the diversion of potential researchers to applied work, although its quality may have benefited from being better focused. Although problems remain, research in this area has a fairly good chance of being useful and of being used. In addition, none of the research issues discussed in the following sections appears to pose any serious methodological difficulties. The conventional experimental methods of the behavioral sciences are suitable for performing the recommended investigations.

RESEARCH ON DECISION MAKING

Given the relatively good communication between decision-making researchers and practitioners, the primary focus of the recommendations that follow is the production of new research, as opposed to its dissemination. It seems reasonable to hope that the same communication networks that brought these applied problems to the attention of academics will carry their partial solutions back to the field. Research on decision making per se assumes that there are general lessons to be learned from studying the sorts of issues that recur in many decision problems and the responses typically made to them. In fact, the complexity of real decision problems is often so great as to prevent some lessons from being learned from direct study.

These recommendations are cast in terms of research needed to improve the use of computerized decision aids, referred to generically as decision analysis. These aids work in an interactive fashion, asking people to provide critical inputs (e.g., the set of actions that they are considering, the probability of those actions achieving various goals), combining those inputs into a recommendation of what action to take, and repeating the process until users feel that they have exhausted its possibilities. In order to be useful, an aid must: (a) deal with those aspects of decision making for which people require assistance, (b) ask for inputs in a language compatible with how people think intuitively about decision making, and (c) display its recommendations in a way that properly captures their implications and definitiveness. Achieving these goals requires understanding of (a) how people assess the quality of human performance in decision-making tasks, (b) the nature of decision-making processes, and (c) how people assess the quality of decision-making processes, both those they perform and those performed for them. The research described below is intended to contribute to all three of these aspects of systems design. It is also intended to facilitate the development of supplementary components of decision-support systems, such as exercises for improving judgment or for more creative option generation.

In this light, research that contributes to hardware or software design should also be a useful adjunct to any formal or semiformal decision-making process in which judgment plays a role. Even the devotee of decision analysis often lacks the time or resources to do anything but an informal analysis.

Decision Structuring

Decision making is commonly characterized as involving the four interrelated steps described earlier. The first three of these give the problem its structure, by specifying the options, facts, and value issues to be considered as well as their interrelations. Prescriptive models of decision making elaborate on the way these steps should be taken. Most descriptive theories hypothesize some deviation of people's practice from a prescriptive model (Fischhoff, Goitein, and Shapira, 1981). These deviations should, in principle, guide the development of the prescriptive model. That is, they show how the prescriptive models fail to consider issues that people want to incorporate in their decisions. In practice, however, the flow of information is typically asymmetrical, with prescriptive models disproportionately setting the tone for descriptive research.

As a result, decision structuring is probably the least developed aspect of research into both prescriptive and descriptive aspects of decision making (von Winterfeldt, 1980). Prescriptive models are typically developed from the pronouncements of economists and others regarding how people should (want to) run their lives or from ad hoc lists of relevant considerations. Descriptive models tend more or less to assume that these prescriptions are correct. Neither seems to have explored fully the range of possible problem representations that people use when left to their own devices.

Paying more attention to the diverse ways in which people do make decisions would enable decision aiders to offer their clients a more diverse set of alternative ways in which they might make decisions, along with some elaboration on the typical strengths and weaknesses of each method. Some research projects that might serve this end follow.

* Studies of dynamic structuring, allowing for iterations in the decision-making process, with each round responding to the insights gained from its predecessors (Humphreys and McFadden, 1980). Can people use such opportunities, or do they tend to stick to an initial representation? Are there initial structures that are less confining, which should be offered by the aids?
* Studies of goals other than narrow optimization. In economic models, the goal of decision making is assumed to be maximizing the utility of the immediate decision. Recently attention has turned to other goals, such as reducing the transaction costs from the act of making a decision, improving trust between the individuals involved in a decision, making do with limited decision-making expertise, imposing consistency over a set of decisions, or facilitating learning from experience. Theoretical studies are needed to clarify the consequences of adopting these goals (e.g., how badly do they sacrifice optimization); empirical studies are needed to see how often people actually want to accept them (particularly after they have been informed of the results of the theoretical studies).
* Option-generation studies. Decision makers can only choose between the options they can think of. Each decision need not be a new test of their imaginations, particularly because research indicates that imagination often fails. Research can suggest better formulation procedures and generic options that can be built into decision analysis schemes (Gettys and Fisher, 1979).
* Many decision analysis schemes are sold as stand-alone systems, to be used by decision makers without the help of a professional decision analyst. The validity of these claims should be tested, particularly with regard to decision structuring, the area in which the largest errors can occur (Pitz, et al., 1980). Research could also show ways to improve the stand-alone capability (e.g., with better introductory training packets).

Measuring Preferences

Unless one is fortunate enough to find a dominating alternative, one that is better than all competitors in all respects, making decisions means making trade-offs. When one cannot have everything, it is necessary to determine the relative importance of different goals. Such balancing acts may be particularly difficult when the question is new and the goals that stand in conflict seem incommensurable (Fischhoff, et al., 1980). Dealing with hazardous technologies, for example, leads us daily to face questions such as whether the benefits of dyeing one's hair are worth a vague, minute increase in the chances of cancer many years hence. Decision analysis schemes seem to complicate life by making these inherent conflicts apparent (McNeil, et al., 1978). They actually complicate it when they pose these questions in cumbersome, unfamiliar ways in order to elicit the information needed by their models--e.g., how great an increase in your probability of being alive in five years' time would exactly compensate for the .20 probability that you will not recover from the proposed surgery--and does this trade-off depend on other factors?

Such questions are difficult in part because their format is dictated by a formal theory or the programmer's convenience, rather than by the decision maker's way of thinking. They are also difficult because of the lack of research guiding their formulation. Research on the elicitation of values has lagged behind research on the elicitation of judgments of fact (Johnson and Huber, 1977). Although there are many highly sophisticated axiomatic schemes for posing value questions, few have been empirically validated for difficult, real-life issues. In practice, perhaps the most common assumption is that decision makers are able to articulate responses to any question that is stated in good English.

The projects described below may help solve problems that currently are (or should be) worrying practitioners. Some similar needs have been identified by the National Research Council's Panel on Survey-Based Measures of Subjective Phenomena (Turner and Martin, in press).

* No opinion. In most behavioral decision research, as in most survey research, economics, and preference theory, people are typically assumed to know what they want. Careful questioning is all that is needed to reveal the decision maker's implicit trade-offs between whatever

goals are being compared. The need for some response is often necessary for the analysis to continue. Knowing how to discover when decision makers have no opinions and how to cope with that situation would be of great value. Studies of "no opinion" in survey research (Schumann and Presser, 1979) would provide a useful base to draw on, although they often show that people have a disturbing ability to manufacture opinions on diverse (and even fictitious) topics.

  • Interactive value measurement. One possible response to situations in which decision makers' values are poorly articulated (or nonexistent) is for the decision aider to engage in a dialogue with the client, suggesting alternative ways of thinking about the problem and the implications of various possible resolutions. Although there are obvious opportunities for manipulating responses in such situations, research may show how they could be minimized; at any rate they may be rendered no worse than the manipulation inherent in not confronting the ambiguity in respondents' values. Of particular interest is the question of whether people are more frank about their values and less susceptible to outside pressures when interacting with a machine than with another human being. Again, some good leads could be found in the survey research literature, particularly in work dealing with the power and prevalence of interviewer effect.

  • Specific topics. In order to interact constructively with their clients, should decision aiders be able to offer a comprehensive, balanced description of the perspectives that one could have on a problem? The provision of such perspectives may be enhanced by a combination of theoretical and empirical work on how people could and do think about particular issues (Jungermann, 1980). For example, to aid decision problems that involve extended time horizons, one would study how people think about good and bad outcomes that are distributed over time. One might discover that people have difficulty conceptualizing distant consequences and therefore tend to discount them unduly; such a tendency could be countered by the use of scenarios that reify hypothetical future experiences. Medical counseling and the setting of safety standards are two other areas with specific problems that reduce the usefulness of decision technologies (e.g., the difficulty of imagining what it would be like to be paralyzed or on dialysis, unwillingness to place a value on human life).

• Simulating values. One obvious advantage of computerized systems is to work quickly through calculations using alternative values of different parameters. A possible didactic use would be to help people clarify what they want, by simulating the implications of different sets of preferences ("If those were your trade-offs, these would be your choices"), both on the problem in question and on sample problems. Work along this line was done at one time in the context of social judgment theory (Hammond, 1971). Completing it and making it accessible to the users of other decision aids would be useful.

• Framing. Recent research has demonstrated that formally equivalent ways of representing decision problems can elicit highly inconsistent preferences (Kahneman and Tversky, 1979; Tversky and Kahneman, 1981). Because most decision-aiding schemes have a typical manner of formulating preference questions, they may inadvertently be biasing the results they produce. This work should be continued, with an eye to characterizing and studying the ways in which decision analysis schemes habitually frame questions.

Evaluation

The decision maker looking for help may be swamped by offers. The range of available options may run from computerized decision analysis routines to super-soft decision therapies. Few of these schemes are supported by empirical validation studies; most are offered by individuals with a vested interest in their acceptance (Fischhoff, 1980). A comprehensive evaluation program would help decision makers sort out the contenders for their attention and to use those selected judiciously, with a full understanding of their strengths and limitations (Wardle and Wardle, 1978). Such a program might involve the following elements:

• Collecting and characterizing the set of existing decision aids with an eye to discerning common behavorial assumptions (e.g., regarding the real difficulties people have in making decisions, the ways in which they want to have problems structured, or the quality of the judgment inputs they can provide to decision-making models).

• Examining the assumptions identified above. This might include questions like: Can people separate judgments of fact from judgments of value? When decision

makers are set to act in the name of an institution, can
they assess its preferences, unencumbered by their own?
Can people introspect usefully about beliefs that have
guided their past decisions, free from the biasing effects
of hindsight?

* Developing methods for evaluating the quality of
decisions (such as are produced by different methods).
For example, what weights should be placed on the quality
of the decision process and on the quality of the outcome
that arises? What level of successful outcomes should be
expected in situations of varying difficulty? This work
would be primarily theoretical (Fischer, 1976).

* Clarifying the method's degree of determinacy.
To what extent do arbitrary changes (i.e., ones regarding
which the method is silent) in mode of application affect
the decisions that arise (Hogarth and Makridakis, 1981)?
Similarly, one would like some general guidance on the
sensitivity of the procedure to changes in various aspects
of the decision-making process, in order to concentrate
efforts on the most important areas (e.g., problem structuring or value elicitation). Conversely, one wants to
know how sensitive the method is to the particulars of
each problem and user. That is, does it tend to render
the same advice in all circumstances?

* Assessing the impact of different methods on
"process" variables, such as the decision maker's alertness to new information that threatens the validity of
the decision analysis or the degree of acceptance that a
procedure generates for the recommendation it produces
(Watson and Brown, 1978). Such questioning of assumptions has been the goal of much existing research, which
should provide a firm data base for new work (although
many questions, such as the first two of the three raised,
have yet to be studied).

Improving Realism

The simplified models of the world that decision analysis
software packages use to represent decision problems are
in at least one key respect very similar to the models
generated by flight or weapons simulators. Their usefulness is constrained by the fidelity of their representations to the critical features of the world they hope to
model. Although there is much speculation about process
effects, it points in inconsistent directions and is
seldom substantiated by empirical studies (either in the

laboratory or in operating organizations). Although these topics have been studied very little in this context, research could draw on whatever analogous studies have been conducted with other kinds of simulators. Some suggested research topics follow.

• Hot and cold cognition. Decision analysis schemes are cold and calculating, and they expect the decision maker to be so as well. It is not clear how well their putative advantages survive when decision makers shift from "cold" to "hot" cognition. Such a shift occurs with emotional involvement, such as might happen when the stakes increase or the topic is arousing (Janis and Mann, 1977). The use of decision aids for medical patients pondering possible treatments assumes that decision quality will not deteriorate in such situations--or at least no more than it deteriorates without the aid. Another such shift involves time pressures, such as might arise in crisis decision making (Wright, 1974). Many proponents of decision analysis claim that time constraints actually enhance the usefulness of their tool, rather than threaten it, arguing that a quick-and-dirty analysis is often the most cost-effective way to use the technology. Evidence is needed regarding whether this is true, both when quickness is chosen and when it is imposed.

• Contingency planning. Many of the most important uses of decision aids are for the sake of contingency planning. The essence of such planning is anticipating future situations and prescribing the actions needed should they actually occur. In principle, preplanning responses should allow a more leisurely and thoughtful analysis with better utilization of experts and decision aids than would be possible if one waited until a situation demanding an immediate response developed. The success of such efforts depends on the planner's ability to imagine in advance how various contingencies will appear should they come about. If the actual contingency does not resemble its image, then the (preplanned) decisions based on that image will seem inappropriate. In such cases, the decision maker must decide on short notice whether to adhere to the plan (and assume that his or her immediate impression is faulty) or come up with a new plan on the spot (and assume that the event that was anticipated is not the event that occurred). Although the stakes riding on contingency plans are often very large, we have little systematic knowledge about the correspondence between actual and planned contingencies. Research is needed on (1) when and why situations look (or feel) different when they occur than they did during planning and (2) what to do when plans made at an earlier time seem inappropriate.

* Overriding recommendations. The moment of truth for the decision aid comes when the decision maker must decide to follow its recommendations or override them. Analogous moments face the users of most other human-machine systems, suggesting that the study of overriding would have broad implications. The research questions are: When do people even think about overriding? How valid are the cues that lead them to do so? How much better than the aid are their intuitive judgments? Does protracted reliance on decision aids increase or decrease intuitive decision-making ability? Existing research on the acceptance of computerized diagnoses in medicine, clinical psychology, and meteorology would provide a good basis for this research.

* Better displays. Decision analysts have shown considerable ingenuity in translating formal decision theory into terms that may be understood by less sophisticated decision makers. More work needs to be done in this area, particularly if decision aids are to have stand-alone capacity. The features that the models capture are a mixture of those that are easy to capture and those that designers intuitively feel are important to include. Each of the four topics just described in this section is a factor that may affect the realism of decision aids and, if so, should be considered in their design and utilization. Research efforts to date have hardly begun to tap the potential of recent work in computer graphics for developing superior displays (e.g., to facilitate interpretation of how robust a recommendation is by showing its susceptibility to change with variation in the values of the input parameters). A particular problem is that both questions and recommendations typically appear without any indication of their rationale. As a result, decision makers may have little feeling for where the questioning is leading or how robust the concluding recommendations will be (or how they can be explained to others). Collaborative efforts might increase both the overall acceptance of decision analysis and the realism of its recommendations when it is used.

Aiding Diffuse Decisions

Common to most decision-making models is the assumption that decisions are made by an identifiable individual at an identifiable point in time. Clearly, however, this idealization often is not realized in practice: there may be many parties to a decision; some decisions just evolve over time (or at least are made to seem that way); other decisions are made by people who do not think of themselves as decision makers (e.g., supervisors monitoring and directing the behavior of subordinates or systems); some decisions are made by people who are not officially recognizable as decision makers (e.g., aides to a senior official). Rather different forms of research are needed to improve decision making in each setting; a number of them are outlined below.

• Multiperson decisions. Decision theory methods are typically designed to explore and aggregate the beliefs and preferences of a single individual. One approach to dealing with multiple decision makers is a computational scheme for aggregating their beliefs and preferences prior to using them in a common decision model (Rohrbaugh, 1979). Theoretical work has suggested a variety of analytical aggregation schemes. Although this work should continue, it could be usefully complemented by empirical studies (using simulations and experimentation) of how greatly the results of these various schemes differ and how well they are accepted by users. Another approach is to have the parties aggregate their perspectives through some structured interaction (Sachman, 1975; Steiner, 1972). This approach, well worked by students of the risky shift and of the Delphi methods, might benefit from research using computerized systems that allow participants (perhaps at different sites) to go through many rounds of interactions with varying communication channels and protocols. For example, will decisions be reached more quickly and adopted more enthusiastically if the parties can observe visual images of one another, not just printed summary statements?

• Evolving decisions. Insofar as decisions represent choices between alternative courses of action, any decision may be expressed as a statement of action ("I [or we] will do X"). Such translation of a complex decision process to its procedural implications can have drawbacks. One is that the underlying rationale of an action is lost, making it difficult to understand why things are done the way they are, how to respond to new contingencies, and when it is time to rethink the whole decision. A second potential drawback is that those decisions that still have to be made are not addressed directly, leaving crucial steps to guesswork (e.g., an operator may be told something to the effect of "Figure out what is going on and then follow steps S_1 to S_n"). A third possibility is that procedures may have internal inconsistencies or be at cross-purposes, and people either do not realize it or they realize it but do not quite know what is wrong. Systems that add rules over time may be particularly prone to this problem (the social security system is an example). Some combination of artificial intelligence, decision modeling, and experimental work might help people to diagnose the logic of the systems that they deal with and that they are called on to redesign (Corbin, 1980; Klein and Weitzenfeld, 1978).

* Unwitting decision makers. Just as any decision may be thought of as an action, so may each action be thought of as a decision. Most students of decision making would probably agree with the hypothesis that people would be better off if they realized the decisions implicit in their actions, and structured them as such. For example, a supervisor contemplating the shutdown of a plant because of a malfunction would make wiser choices with even a rudimentary decision analysis (i.e., listing all possible courses of action, sketching out possible consequences and contingencies, crudely working through the expected utility of each action). Such structuring has become part of the training of some medical students. The user of computerized information retrieval systems (e.g., Prestel, Teletext) might be usefully seen as making a series of decisions (such as: These alternatives are ambiguous--which gives me the best chance of getting the information I need? Is it worth my time and money to use the system on this problem? Is the answer I got complete enough or should I keep working?). A useful way to exploit existing research would be to translate it into crude aids, adapted to the conditions and problems of particular work settings (along with an evaluation of their efficacy).

* Unofficial decision makers. Senior officials in many organizations are too busy to make deliberative analyses of the many decisions they must consider. A common (and sensible) defense is to have aides conduct the analyses. For this strategem to work, the senior

official must communicate well enough with the aide to ensure that the appropriate problem is addressed; the aide must communicate well enough with the senior official to ensure that the rationale behind the decision-making method and the implications of its conclusions are understood well enough to be properly represented and afforded due consideration. Communication problems are likely to be particularly great when the official must present the conclusions to some larger public or when the training of official and aide are quite different. Consider, for example, the difficulties experienced by public officials enunciating the policies devised by economists or by those of junior executives trying to sell decision analyses to old-line senior executives. Better methods of communication (and for realizing the lack of it) would be a useful addition to the software accompanying any decision-making method. These methods could apply to the front end of an analysis (e.g., training films, practice exercises) or after it is complete (Federico, et al., 1980).

CONCLUSION

Decision aiding appears to be increasingly viable and popular. A variety of software packages are currently being marketed and used, each offering somewhat different operationalizations of the basic model. If their promises are not to outstrip their capabilities, they will need to be accompanied by behavorial research regarding how best to design and use that software. The five problem areas described in this chapter represent topics for which research is likely to be particularly useful and usable.

These projects require primarily experimental methods, building on the theory and hardware already available. To be most effective they need a context that affords ready contact with decision theorists and practicing decision analysts. The former can solve the questions of theory to which they are most suited; the latter can provide access to their machines (and perhaps to their clients) and facilitate the translation from research to practice.

REFERENCES

Bonczek, R. H., Holsapple, C. U., and Whinston, A. B.
   1981   <u>Foundations of Decision Support Systems</u>. New York: Academic Press.

Brown, R., Kahr, A. S., and Peterson, C.
 1974 *Decisional Analysis for the Manager*. New York: Holt, Rinehart & Winston.

Corbin, R.
 1980 Decisions that might not get made. In T. Wallsten, ed., *Cognitive Processes in Choice and Decision Behavior*. Hillsdale, N. J.: Lawrence Erlbaum.

Einhorn, H., and Hogarth, R. M.
 1981 Behavorial decision theory: processes of judgment and choice. *Annual Review of Psychology* 32:53-88.

Federico, P. A., Brun, K. E., and McCalla, D. B.
 1980 *Management Information Systems and Organization Behavior*. New York: Praeger.

Fischer, G. W.
 1976 Multidimensional utility models for risky and riskless choice. *Organizational Behavior and Human Performance* 17:127-146.

Fischhoff, B.
 1980 Clinical decision analysis. *Operations Research* 28:28-43.

Fischhoff, B., Goitein, B., and Shapira, Z.
 1981 The experienced utility of expected utility approaches. In N. Feather, ed., *Expectancy, Incentive and Action*. Hillsdale, N. J.: Lawrence Erlbaum.

Fischhoff, B., Lichtenstein, S., Slovic, P., Derby, S., and Keeney, R.
 1981 *Acceptable Risk*. New York: Cambridge University Press.

Fischhoff, B., Slovic, P., and Lichtenstein, S.
 1980 Knowing what you want: measuring labile values. In T. S. Wallsten, ed., *Cognitive Processes in Choice and Decision Behavior*. Hillsdale, N. J.: Lawrence Erlbaum.

Gettys, C. F. and Fisher, S. D.
 1979 Hypothesis plausibility and hypothesis generation. *Organizational Behavior and Human Performance* 24:93-110.

Hammond, K. R.
 1971 Computer graphics as an aid to learning. *Science* 172:903-908.

Hogarth, R. M. and Makridakis, S.
 1981 Forcecasting and planning: an evaluation. *Management Science* 27:115-138.

Humphreys, D., and McFadden, W.
  1980 Experiences with MAUD: aiding decision structuring versus bootstrapping the decision maker. *Acta Psychologica* 45:51-69.

Janis, I. L., and Mann, L.
  1977 *Decision Making.* New York: Free Press.

Johnson, E. M., and Huber, G. P.
  1977 The technology of utility assessment. *IEEE Transactions on Systems Management & Cybernetics* SMC-7:311-325.

Jungermann, H.
  1980 Speculations about decision-theoretic aids for personal decision making. *Acta Psychologica* 45:7-34.

Kahneman, D., and Tversky, A.
  1979 Prospect theory. *Econometrica* 47:263-292.

Klein, G. A., and Weitzenfeld, J.
  1978 Improvement of skills for solving ill-defined problems. *Educational Psychology* 13:31-41.

McNeil, B. J., Weichselbaum, R., and Pauker, S. G.
  1978 Fallacy of the 5-year survival rate in lung cancer. *New England Journal of Medicine* 299:1397-1401.

Pitz, G. F., Sachs, N. J., and Heerboth, M. T.
  1980 Structure for individual decision analysis. *Organizational Behavior & Human Performance* 26:65-80.

Raiffa, H.
  1968 *Decision Analysis.* Reading, Mass.: Addison-Wesley.

Rohrbaugh, J.
  1979 Improving the quality of group judgment. *Organizational Behavior and Human Performance* 24:73-92.

Sachman, H.
  1975 *Delphi Critique.* Lexington, Mass.: Lexington Books.

Sage, A. P.
  1981 Behavorial and organizational considerations in the design of information systems and processes for planning and decision support. *IEEE Transactions on Systems Management and Cybernetics* SMC-11:640-678.

Schumann, H., and Presser, S.
  1979 Assessment of no opinion in attitude surveys. *Sociological Methodology* 10:241-275.

Slovic, P., Fischhoff, B., and Lichtenstein, S.
   1979   Behavioral decision theory. *Annual Review of Psychology* 28:1-39.

Steiner, I. D.
   1972   *Group Processes and Production*. New York: Academic Press.

Svenson, O.
   1979   Process descriptions of decision making. *Organizational Behavior & Human Performance* 23:86-112.

Turner, C., and Martin, E.
   in press   *Surveying Subjective Phenomena*. Panel on Survey-Based Measures of Subjective Phenomena, Committee on National Statistics, National Research Council. New York: Russell Sage.

Tversky, A., and Kahneman, D.
   1981   The framing of the decisions and the psychology of choice. *Science* 211:456-458.

von Winterfeldt, D.
   1980   Structuring decision problems for decision analysis. *Acta Psychologica* 45:71-93.

Wallsten, T.
   1980   *Cognitive Processes in Choice and Decision Behavior*. Hillsdale, N. J.: Lawrence Erlbaum.

Wardle, A., and Wardle, L.
   1978   Computer-aided diagnosis—a review of research. *Methods of Information in Medicine* 17:15-28.

Watson, S. R., and Brown, R. V.
   1978   The valuation of decision analysis. *Journal of the Royal Statistical Society* Series A(141):69-78.

Wright, P.
   1974   The harassed decision maker. *Journal of Applied Psychology* 59:555-561.

3

ELICITING INFORMATION FROM EXPERTS

Many formal and informal processes in working organizations hinge on the effective communication of "expert information." Risk analyses may require a metallurgist to assess the likelihood of a valve's fracturing under an anticipated stress or a human factors expert to assess the likelihood of its failing to open due to faulty maintenance. Strategic analyses may require substantive experts to assess the growth rate of the Soviet economy or the proportion of its expenditures directed to arms. Tactical planning in marketing or the military may demand real-time reports by field personnel of what seems to be happening "at the front." Air traffic control typically requires succinct, unambiguous status reports from all concerned. Computerized career-counseling routines or procedures for establishing entitlement to social benefits assume that lay people can report on those aspects of their own lives about which they are the ranking experts. The U.S. Census Bureau makes similar assumptions when asking people about their employment status, as a step toward directing federal policies and jobs programs. In product liability trials technical experts give evidence in a highly stylized manner.

As can be seen from these examples, experts may talk to the consumers of their advice directly, to elicitors who then translate what they say into a form usable by a computer, or to a computer. Insofar as computers have been designed by people, all of these communication modes assume some fairly high level of interpersonal understanding. The elicitors must ask questions that people can sensibly answer. The recipients of those answers

---

The principal author of this chapter is Baruch Fischhoff.

must interpret them with an appreciation of the errors and ambiguities they may conceal. The quality of that communication is likely to depend on the novelty of the problems, the historic level of interaction between questioner and answerer, and the quickness with which miscommunications produce diagnostic signs. Poor elicitation by air traffic controllers may become visible very quickly; whereas employment surveys may (and have) elicited biased responses and misdirected economic planning for years without the error's being detected. Particularly clumsy elicitation may lead users to reject the eliciting system, thereby avoiding mistakes but also wasting the resources that have been invested in its design.

New research about elicitation and the translation of existing research findings into more usable form could benefit a wide variety of enterprises. As this chapter discusses, elicitation is not a field of inquiry or application in and of itself, but a function that recurs in many problems. This creates special difficulties for the accumulation and dissemination of knowledge about it.

BACKGROUND

Perhaps because elicitation is a part of many problems but all of none, it has emerged neither as a discipline nor as an area that is seen to require special expertise. The typical assumption is that elicitation is not a particular problem, as long as things stay fairly simple and one uses common sense. The validity of that assumption may not be questioned until some egregious problem has clearly arisen from a particular failure. When problems arise, the lack of a coherent body of knowledge may encourage ad hoc solutions, with little systematic testing or accumulation of knowledge. Solutions are generated from the resources of those working on a particular problem and viewed from their narrow perspective.

One reason for aggregating these elicitation issues into a single chapter is to keep them from being orphaned, as parts of many problems for which there is no focus of responsibility. Another reason is to suggest that there are enough recurrent themes to generate a coherent body of knowledge, thereby reducing the degree to which each system designer faced with an elicitation problem must start from scratch. Although work may still focus on specific problems, conceptualizing them in a general way may increase both the pool of talent they draw on and the breadth of perspective with which their solutions are interpreted and reported. Because a common element of these projects is dealing with substantive experts, their cumulative impact should be to generate a better understanding of the judgmental processes of experts.

The research bases for the following projects are sufficiently diverse that further details are given within each context. In some cases, there is a distinct research literature on which new projects can be based. In others, the proposed topic does not exist as a separate pursuit, or at least not within the context of human factors; the literature cited is suggestive of the kinds of approaches that have proven useful in other fields or related problems that might be drawn on.

RESEARCH ON ELICITATION

Ensuring a Common Frame of Reference

An obvious precondition for communication is ensuring that elicitor and respondent are talking about the same thing. In ordinary conversation the participants have some opportunity for detecting and rectifying misunderstandings. If questions are set down once for all respondents, then misunderstandings must be anticipated in advance. Some implicit theory of potential (mis)interpretations must guide the question composers for management systems, accident report forms, or automatic diagnostic routines that rely on expert judgment.

These problems are not, of course, unique to human factors. They are probably best understood by professionals whose central concern for the longest periods of time has been asking questions; these include anthropologists (Agar, 1980), linguists, historians (Hexter, 1971), survey researchers (Payne, 1952), philosophers, and some social psychologists (Rosenthal and Rosnow, 1969). Two general conclusions that one can derive from their work is that the opportunities for misinterpretation are much greater than most people would presuppose and that the nature of possible specific misinterpretations is hard to imagine intuitively.

The chances for miscommunication are likely to increase to the extent that elicitor and respondent come from different cultures and have had little opportunity to interact. Systems designed by technical experts for lay users often fall into this category, especially when the elicitation is far removed physically or temporally from the design effort. Consider, for example, a computerized job search program that requires unemployed workers to characterize their experience in terms of one of the 12,000 categories of the Dictionary of Occupational Titles (DOT) code (e.g., handkerchief presser). Although a considerable intellectual effort has gone into imposing a semblance of order on the world of work, that order may be very poorly matched to the way in which applicants conceptualize their experience. Indeed, even those who elicit such information from job applicants and translate it into the DOT code on a full-time basis may have considerable difficulty. Similar problems may face a system designed to clarify entitlement to social services or a computerized system for diagnosing car or radio problems on the basis of a user's description of presenting symptoms. These problems may persist even with the clearest display and the most lucid users' manual.

Although the details of each problem are unique, seeing their common elements can enable designers to exploit a larger body of existing research and research methods. One strategy is literature reviews that make accessible the methods used by fields such as anthropology to uncover misunderstandings. Using these methods with small samples of users prior to designing systems or in the early stages of design could effectively suggest minor changes or even major issues (such as whether the system could ever stand alone, or whether it will always need an interpreter between it and the actual user). Such strategies are increasingly being used in survey design; they may even lead to some revision in the categories of Justice Department statistics so as to make them more compatible with the ways in which victims of crimes think about their experience (National Research Council, 1976).

Another research strategy is to review existing case studies of mishaps (e.g., in diplomacy, survey research, police work, or software design) for evidence of problems due to questioners and respondents unwittingly speaking different languages (Brooks and Bailar, 1978). Such studies would help establish the prevalence of such problems and create a stock of cautionary tales for educational and motivational purposes.

A third strategy involves experimental and observational studies of groups of individuals who regularly communicate with one another, in order to see how well they understand one another's perspectives. Software designers and less educated users, engineers and machine operators, and market researchers and consumers are a few such dyads. The intuitive beliefs of the elicitors in each of these dyads regarding the perspectives of their respondents might provide some productive hypotheses and reveal some misconceptions worthy of correction.

Better ways of eliciting information should also suggest better ways of presenting it. Informing and counseling patients about medical risks is one area in which these problems are currently under active study (see Chapter 2).

Matching Questions to Mental Structures

A presumption of many elicitation efforts is that the respondent has an answer to any question that the elicitor can raise (Turner and Martin, in press). One contributing factor to this belief is the fact that elicitors often cannot accept "no answer" for an answer, needing some best guess at the answer in order to get on with business. A second contributing factor may be the tendency, long known to surveyors, for respondents to offer opinions on even nonexistent issues, perhaps reflecting some feeling that they can, should, or must have opinions on everything. A third factor may be the elicitors' (intuitive or scientific) models of memory that presume a coherent store of knowledge waiting to be tapped by whatever question proves most useful to the elicitor (Lindley, et al., 1979).

Coping with situations in which the respondent has little or no knowledge about the topic in question is dealt with in the next section, on how to elicit assessments of information quality. Alternatively, the respondent may have the needed information, but not in the form required by the question. Whenever there is incompatibility between the way in which knowledge is organized and the way in which it is elicited, the danger arises that the expert may not be used to best advantage, may provide misleading information, or may be seduced into doing a task to which his or her expertise does not extend. For example, risk assessment programs often require the designers of a technical system to describe it in terms of the logical interrelationships between various components (including its human operators, repair people, suppliers, etc.) and to assess the probability of these components' failing at various rates, perhaps as a function of several variables (Jennergren and Keeney, 1981).

Given these judgmental inputs, these programs may perform miraculous simulations and calculations; however, the value of such analyses is contingent on the quality of the judgments. The processes by which experts are recruited may or may not take into consideration the need for these special skills. In some situations, no one may have them.

Research designed to improve the compatibility of questions with the way in which knowledge is stored should be guided by substantive theories about that storage as well as practical knowledge of the information needed. The citations given here represent different approaches to conceptualizing such mismatches between precise questions and differently organized or unorganized knowledge. As an example of the kinds of testable hypotheses that emerge from these literatures, consider the possibility that many experts experience the topics of their expertise one by one, whereas elicitors often need a summary (e.g., of the rate of target detections by sonar operators, the conditional probability of misreading an altimeter given a particular number of hours of flying experience, the distribution of hearing deficits associated with various noise levels). If experts are not accustomed to aggregating their experience, then they will respond differently to procedures that request aggregate estimates immediately and those that focus first (and perhaps entirely) on the recall of individual incidents (Fischhoff and Whipple, 1981). This particular research could build somewhat on probability learning studies or attempts to distinguish between episodic and semantic memory.

Efforts to design the best response mode assume that respondents have the knowledge that the elicitor needs, but not organized in the most convenient form. A more troublesome situation arises when they do not have it organized at all. In that case the elicitor's task becomes to evoke all of the relevant bits and pieces, then devise some scheme for interpreting them. Doing so first requires discovering that incoherence exists, which may not be easy, insofar as a set of questions may elicit consistent responses simply because it has consistently imposed one of several possible perspectives. Although sensitive elicitors may already be poking around creatively, there are few codified and tested procedures. Such procedures might involve standard sets of questions designed to produce diverse perspectives, which the respondent would then integrate to provide a best guess (or set of best guesses) for the problem at hand. For example, one might always ask about case-by-case and aggregate estimates, in that order. Such efforts might also prompt and be helped by the development of memory models allowing for multiple, incoherent representations.

Clarifying Information Quality

Before taking action on an expert's opinion, one wants to know how good that best guess is. Great uncertainty might prompt one to try to uncover its sources or to take alternative courses of action (e.g., hedging one's bets). Although explicit assessments of uncertainty are becoming a greater part of enterprises such as risk analysis (Fairley, 1977), weather forecasting (Murphy and Winkler, 1977), and strategic assessment (Daly and Andriole, 1980), such experiences are rare for most people. As one would expect in novel elicitation situations, the responses that people give are not always to be trusted. Assessments of information quality (or confidence or probability) have been the subject of extensive research over the last decade (Lichtenstein, et al., 1982). It has produced a fairly robust set of methods for eliciting uncertainty and a moderately good understanding of human performance in this regard. The clearest finding is that people have a partial but not complete appreciation of the extent of their own knowledge. Most commonly, this partial knowledge expresses itself in overconfidence, which seems quite impervious to most attempts at debiasing, except for intensive training (Fischhoff, 1982).

Many practical problems could be solved in this area with a moderate investment in completing the research that has already been started. This research could use the stock of elicitation techniques already available to understand better the range and potency of overconfidence biases, to clarify how worrisome they are, and to determine the most effective training and how far it can be generalized. Of particular interest is the extent to which experts are prone to these problems when making judgments in their areas of expertise; current evidence suggests that they are, but it is still inconclusive given the importance of the question (Spetzler and Stael von Holstein, 1975).

The practical steps that can be taken subsequent to such research are developing and testing training procedures, identifying the least bias-prone elicitation methods for situations in which training is impossible or ineffective, and anticipating the extent of bias with different methods and situations in order to apply ad hoc corrections. Choosing between these steps and implementing them efficiently will require a more detailed understanding of the cognitive processes involved in representing and integrating probabilistic information. Although existing research covers much of the ground between basic cognitive psychology and field applications, it has not quite touched bases with either extreme. Coping with this practical problem might provoke some interesting theoretical work in the representation of knowledge.

Eliciting Systems

In the examples used in the preceding sections, the knowledge that experts were asked to provide dealt with the components of some large system (e.g., a failure probability, a job choice, a burnout rate). At times, however, experts are required to describe the entire system (Hayes-Roth, et al., 1981). Software packages that attempt to elicit a big picture include some of those used in decision structuring, failure probability modeling (U.S. Nuclear Regulatory Commission, 1981), map making, route planning, and economic analysis. Once such systems have been programmed well enough to work at all, one must ascertain the degree of fidelity between the representations they produce and the conceptual or physical systems they are meant to model; attempts to develop better elicitation methods or to cope with known limits or errors should follow (Brown and Van Lehn, 1980). The research strategies outlined below, based in part on the initial work already begun and in part on discussions with troubled system elicitors, may shed some light on these problems. In each case one would want to know whether a change in procedure made a difference and, if so, whether one method would be preferred in some or all situations. Because so little systematic knowledge is available on how results may vary with different elicitation procedures, generalizing the existing research findings should be done cautiously.

• Determining whether formally equivalent ways of eliciting the same information produce different responses. For example, a category of events may be judged differently when considered as a whole and when disaggregated into component categories.

* Evaluating the effectiveness of methods that require more and less "deep" (or analytical or inferential) judgments about system operation. For example, if a process produces a distribution of events (e.g., failure rates), one could assess that distribution directly or judge something about the data-generating process.

* Varying the amount of feedback provided about how the elicited system operates. For example, when a simulation of an industrial process is designed according to an expert's judgment, it may be run a few times, just to see if it produces more or less sensible results. The expert could then introduce apparently needed adjustments. Such tinkering should lead to successive improvements in the model; however, it can also prevent simulations from producing nonintuitive (i.e., surprising, informative) results. It also threatens the putative independence of the models created by different experts in areas such as climatology and macroeconomics. The convergence of these models' predictions (about the future of the economy, for example) is used as a sign of their validity. In practice, however, econometricians monitor one another's models and adjust theirs if they produce outlying predictions.

* Assessing experts' ability to judge the completeness of a representation. How well can they tell whether all important components have been included? Available evidence suggests that considerations that are out of sight are also out of mind; once experts have begun to think about a model in a particular way, the accessibility of other perspectives is appreciably reduced (Fischhoff, et al., 1978). If this is generally true, an elicitor might try to evoke a variety of perspectives on the system superficially before pursuing any in depth (as a sort of intra-expert brainstorming).

Estimating Numerical Quantities

A common form of uncertainty is knowing something about a topic, but not a necessary fact. If that fact is a number (e.g., the number of tanks an enemy has or the percentage of those tanks that are in operating order), it may be possible to use the related facts in a systematic way if one can devise a rule or algorithm for composing them (Armstrong, 1977). The validity of such estimates depends on the appropriateness of the algorithms, the quality of the component estimates, and the accuracy of their composition. Used appropriately, algorithms can make otherwise impenetrable judgmental processes explicit and subject both to external criticism and to self-improvement, as one can systematically update one's best estimate whenever more is learned about any component (Singer, 1971).

Although there are many advocates of algorithmic thinking and anecdotal evidence of its power, there do not seem to be many empirical studies of their usefulness (Hogarth and Makridakis, 1981). Such studies of algorithm efficacy as do exist seem concentrated on the solving of deterministic logical problems for which all relevant evidence is presented to the respondent and a clear criterion of success exists, rather than estimation tasks in which the accuracy of the estimate will be unclear until some external validation is provided. Like any other judgmental technique, algorithmic thinking could be more trouble than it is worth if it increases confidence in judgment more than it improves judgment.

A primary research project here would be to compile a set of plausible and generally applicable algorithmic strategies. Process tracing of the judgmental processes of expert estimators might be one source. The algorithms discovered in the study of logical problem solving might be another. A subsequent project could attempt to teach people to use these algorithms, then, looking at the fidelity with which they can be applied, measure the accuracy of their results and their influence on confidence. The use of multiple algorithms and people's ability to correct the results of imperfect algorithms are also worth study. The best algorithms could then become part of management information systems, decision support systems, and the like.

Two interpretive literature reviews might provide useful adjuncts to this research. One would look at work on mental arithmetic of the sort required when people must execute algorithms in their heads. Although computational devices should be able to eliminate the need for such exercises, judges may still be caught without their tools or may use unwritten mini-algorithms in order to produce component estimates (once they've gotten the general idea). The second review would summarize, in a form accessible to designers, the psychophysics literature on stimulus-presentation and response-mode effects (Poulton, 1977). That literature shows the degree of variability in magnitude estimation that can arise from "artifactual" changes in procedure (e.g., order of alternative presentation, kind of numbers used).

Detecting Reporting Bias

The preceding sections have assumed that elicitor and respondent are engaged in an honest, unconflicted attempt to produce a best estimate of some quantity or relationship. When research identifies difficulties, one assumes a mutual good faith effort on the part of elicitors and experts to eliminate them. In the real world, however, many wrong answers are deliberate; their producers do not wish to have them either detected or corrected. If the citations given here are at all representative, systematic misrepresentation has been of greatest interest to those concerned with the social and economic context within which behavior takes place. Such misrepresentations may be usefully divided into two categories. The first includes deliberate attempts to deceive in order to gain some advantage. For example, economists chronically mistrust verbal reports of people's preferences (i.e., surveys) for fear that respondents engage in strategic behavior, trying to "put one over" on the questioner and distort the survey's results (Brookshire, et al., 1976). Some critics of survey research are even advocating that respondents do so deliberately so as to stop the survey juggernaut (see Turner and Martin, in press), as do some people in organizations who feel threatened by computerized information systems and wish to see them fail.

The second category of misreports reflects cultural or subcultural norms. In a business or military unit, for example, optimism (or grousing) may be the norm for communication between members of some ranks (Tihansky, 1976). Or there may be a norm of exaggerating one's wealth or weight. Those who share the norms know how to recode the spoken word to gain a more accurate assessment; however, mechanical systems designed by people outside the culture may take those reports at face value and thereby introduce systematic errors into their workings.

Although investigating misreporting is likely to be quite difficult, identifying it is part of systems design. One way to start is to review the relevant literature in fields that have dealt with these questions (e.g., sociology, economics). A second is to interview experts off the record about how (and how often) they try to manipulate systems that pose questions to them. A third is to observe ongoing elicitations for which it is possibile to validate responses.

Difficulties, once identified, must still be treated. One method is to institute penalties for misreporting. A second is to make consistency checks to detect errors. A third is to eliminate the reasons for misreporting (e.g., ensuring confidentiality). A fourth is to correct misreports for known biases. For example, the Central Electricity Generating Board in Great Britain discovered that it could quite accurately predict the time needed to return a power station to operation by doubling the time estimates reported by the chief plant engineers. One difficulty with such adjustments is that people may change their reporting practices if they find out about them (Kidd, 1970).

Reporting Past Events

Many planning and design activities are heavily guided by reports of past events, particularly accidents or other failures (Petzoldt, 1977; Rasmussen, 1980). One reconstructs the way in which a system should have operated, contrasts that with the way in which it actually operated, and uses that comparison to improve future design (perhaps assigning guilt and enacting penalties along the way).

Such retrospections are inevitably colored by the reporter's knowledge of what has happened. As common sense suggests and the citations below partially document, that coloring can be the source of needed detail or of systematic distortion. It has been found, for example, that people seem to exaggerate in hindsight what could have been (and was) known in foresight; they use explanatory schemes so complicated and so poorly specified as to defy empirical test; they remember people as having been more like their present selves than was actually the case; they fail to remember crucial acts that they themselves performed. These problems seem to afflict both the garden-variety retrospections evoked in laboratory studies and those of professional historians, strategic analysts, and eyewitnesses (Fischhoff, 1975).

One needed project is to make these studies available to those engaged in eliciting or using retrospective reports. Another is to attempt to replicate them in human factors domains. Of particular interest are cases in which the direction of bias has been documented sufficiently to allow recalibration of biased retrospections. In cases in which distortions are less predictable, techniques should be developed to help experts reconstruct their view of the situation before, during, and after the event. For example, such research may show that people exaggerate the probability they assigned (or would have assigned) to past events before they occurred by about 20 percent, on the average. That knowledge may make it possible to adjust retrospective probability assessments, but not to eliminate distortions in the way particular events and causal links are drawn.

For assigning blame or understanding how an accident situation looked to an operator just before things started to go wrong, strict (accurate) reconstruction is essential. For understanding how the system actually operates, one needs to be wary of the danger that experts have learned too much from a particular event, thereby misinterpreting the importance and generality of the causal forces involved. Generals who prepare for the last war may fit this stereotype, as may the operators of supervisory control systems who respond to each mishap by ensuring that it will not happen again, then rest confident that the system as a whole is now fail-safe.

Three research strategies appear to offer some promise for clarifying these questions. One is to review the reports of historians, judges, journalists, and others about how they detect and avoid biases. A second is to do theory-based experiments, looking at how memory accommodates new information, particularly to see which processes are reversible. The third is research on debiasing, looking at the effect of directly warning people, of raising the stakes riding on a decision, or of instructing them to change the structure of the task to one that uses their intellectual skills to better advantage.

CONCLUSION

Eliciting information from experts successfully is important to a variety of systems and organizations. The care taken in elicitation varies greatly, from detailed studies of the elicitation of some specific recurrent judgments, to careful deliberations unsupported by empirical research, to casual solutions. Even though elicitation is not a discipline per se, research such as that suggested in this chapter could focus more attention on it and make a body of knowledge accessible to designers. In part, that knowledge would be borrowed from related fields (with suitable translations); in part it would be created expressly to solve human factors problems. Some of these projects could be undertaken in their own right; others would be best developed as part of ongoing projects, with more emphasis on elicitation than might otherwise be the case. The interdisciplinary aspect of many projects may generate interest in human factors problems on the part of workers in other fields (e.g., memory representation, workplace culture), and their expertise could contribute to human factors research.

REFERENCES

Agar, M.
   1980   The Intimate Stranger. New York: Academic Press.

Armstrong, J. S.
   1977   Long Range Forecasting. New York: Wiley.

Brooks, A., and Bailar, B. A.
   1978   An Error Profile: Employment as Measured by the Current Population Survey. Statistical Policy Working Paper 3. Washington, D.C.: U.S. Department of Commerce.

Brookshire, D. S., Ives, B. C., and Schulze, W. D.
   1976   The valuation of aesthetic preferences. Journal of Environmental Economics and Management 3:325-346.

Brown, J. S., and Van Lehn, K.
   1980   Repair theory: a generative theory of bugs in procedural skills. Cognitive Science 4:379-426.

Daly, J. A., and Andriole, S. J.
   1980   The use of events/interaction research by the intelligence community. Policy Sciences 12:215-236.

Fairley, W. B.
   1977   Evaluating the "small" probability of a catastrophic accident from the marine transportation of liquefied natural gas. In W. B. Fairley and F. Mosteller, eds., Statistics and Public Policy. Reading, Mass.: Addison-Wesley.

Fischhoff, B.
   1982   Debiasing. In D. Kahneman, P. Slovic, and A. Tversky, eds., Judgment Under Uncertainty: Heuristics and Biases. New York: Cambridge University Press.

Fischhoff, B.
    1975   Hindsight ≠ foresight: the effect of outcome knowledge on judgment under uncertainty. Journal of Experimental Psychology: Human Perception and Performance 1:288-299.

Fischhoff, B., Slovic, P., and Lichtenstein, S.
    1978   Fault trees: sensitivity of estimated failure probabilities to problem representation. Journal of Experimental Psychology: Human Perception and Performance 4:330-344.

Fischhoff, B., and Whipple, C.
    1981   Risk assessment: evaluating errors in subjective estimates. The Environmental Professional 3:272-281.

Hexter, J. H.
    1971   The History Primer. New Haven: Yale University Press.

Hogarth, R. M., and Makridakis, S.
    1981   Forecasting and planning: an appraisal. Management Science 27:115-138.

Jennergren, L. P., and Keeney, R. L.
    1981   Risk assessment. In Handbook of Applied System Analysis. Laxenburg, Austria: International Institute of Applied Systems Analysis.

Kidd, J. B.
    1970   The utilization of subjective probabilities in production planning. Acta Psychologica 34:338-347.

Lichtenstein, S., Fischhoff, B., and Philips, L. D.
    1982   Calibration of probabilities: state of the art to 1980. In D. Kahneman, P. Slovic, and A. Tversky, eds., Judgment Under Uncertainty: Heuristics and Biases. New York: Cambridge University Press.

Lindley, D. V., Tversky, A., and Brown, R. V.
    1979   On the reconciliation of probability assessments. Journal of the Royal Statistical Society. Series A(142) Part 2:146-180.

Murphy, A. H., and Winkler, R.
    1977   Can weather forecasters formulate reliable probability forecasts of precipitation and temperature? National Weather Digest 2:2-9.

National Research Council
    1976   Surveying Crime. Panel for the Evaulation of Crime Surveys, Committee on National Statistics. Washington, D.C.: National Academy of Sciences.

Payne, S. L.
   1952   The Art of Asking Questions. Princeton, N.
           J.: Princeton University Press.
Pezoldt, V. J.
   1977   Rare Event/Accident Research Methodology.
           Washington, D.C.: National Bureau of
           Standards.
Poulton, E. C.
   1977   Quantitative subjective assessments are almost
           always biased, sometimes completely
           misleading. British Journal of Psychology
           68:409-425.
Rasmussen, J.
   1980   What can be learned from human error reports.
           In K. D. Duncan, M. Gruneberg, and D. Wallis,
           eds., Changes in Working Life. New York:
           Wiley.
Rosenthal, R., and Rosnow, R.
   1969   Artifact in Experimental Design. New York:
           Academic Press.
Singer, M.
   1971   The vitality of mythical numbers. The Public
           Interest 23:3-9.
Spetzler, C. S., and Stael von Holstein, C-A.
   1975   Probability encoding in decision analysis.
           Management Science 22:340-358.
Tihansky, D.
   1976   Confidence assessment of military air frame
           cost predictions. Operations Research
           24:26-43.
Turner, C. and Martin, E., eds.
   in   Surveying Subjective Phenomena. Panel on
   press   Survey-Based Measures of Subjective Phenomena,
           Committee on National Statistics, National
           Research Council. New York: Russell Sage.
U.S. Nuclear Regulatory Commission
   1981   Fault Tree Handbook. Washington, D.C.: U.S.
           Nuclear Regulatory Commission.
Waterman, D., and Hayes-Roth, F.
   1982   An Investigation of Tools for Building Expert
           Systems. Report prepared for the National
           Science Foundation. Santa Monica, Calif:
           Rand Corporation.

4
SUPERVISORY CONTROL SYSTEMS

In the past 15 years the introduction of automation into working environments has created more and more jobs in which operators are given very high levels of responsibility and very little to do. The degree of responsibility and the amount of work vary from position to position, but the defining properties of such jobs are: (1) The operator has overall responsibility for control of a system that, under normal operating conditions, requires only occasional fine tuning of system parameters in order to maintain satisfactory performance. (2) The major tasks are to program changes in inputs or control routines and to serve as a backup in the case of a failure or malfunction in a system component. (3) Important participation in system operation occurs infrequently and at unpredictable times. (4) The time constraints associated with participation, when it occurs, can be very short, of the order of a few seconds or minutes. (5) The values and costs associated with operator decisions can be very large. (6) Good performance requires rapid assimilation of large quantities of information and the exercise of relatively complex inference processes.

These kinds of jobs are found in the process control industries, such as chemical plants and nuclear power plants. They are involved in the control of aircraft, ships, and urban rapid transit systems, robotic remote control systems for inspection and manipulation in the deep ocean, and computer-aided manufacturing. They are involved in medical patient-monitoring systems and law

---

The principal authors of this chapter are Thomas B. Sheridan, Baruch Fischhoff, Michael Posner, and Richard W. Pew.

enforcement information and control systems. As computer aids are introduced into military command and control systems, such jobs become involved in that area. For example, the Army alone currently has 70 automated or computer-aided systems at the concept development stage (U.S. Army Research Institute, 1979). The other services have similar projects under development.

The human factors problems involved in supervisory control systems can be classifed into five categories.

1. <u>Display</u>. In the past these systems have used large arrays of meters and gauges or large situation boards and control panels to display information, with the general goal of displaying everything, because one never knows exactly what will be needed. Little attention has been paid to the need to assimilate diverse information sources into coherent patterns for making inferences simply and directly. Today computers are being used more and more in the control of these operations; large display panels are being collapsed into computer-generated displays that can call up the needed information on demand. These developments in physical technology are pushing human factors engineers to devise better ways of coding and formating large collections of information to facilitate interpretation and reliable decisions by operators. Also needed are better means of accessing information, means that are not opaque and do not leave operators confused in urgent and stressful situations.

2. <u>Command</u>. The emergence of powerful computers and robotic devices has necessitated the development of better "command languages," by which operators can convey instructions to a lower-level intelligence, perhaps giving examples or hints and providing criteria or preferences, and doing it in a communication mode that is natural and adaptable to different people and linguistic styles.

3. <u>Operator's Model</u>. We also lack well-developed methodologies for identifying the internal conceptual model on the basis of which an operator attempts to solve a problem. (This has also been called the operator's system image, picture, or problem space.) Incorrect operator's models can lead to disastrous results (e.g., Three Mile Island); it is obviously a matter of utmost importance for operators of military command and control systems to acquire proper conceptual models and keep them updated on a moment-by-moment basis in times of crisis.

4. Workload. We have no good principles of job design for operations in supervisory control systems, in part because it has proved extremely difficult to measure or estimate the mental workloads involved. They tend to be highly transient, varying from light and boring when the work is routine to extremely demanding when action is critical. At present there is no consensus on what mental workload is or how to measure it, especially in the context of supervisory control.

5. Proficiency and Error. Issues of training and proficiency maintenance are critical in this kind of operation because each event is in some sense unique and is drawn from an extremely large set of possibilities, most of which will never occur during the operating life of the system. It is not easy to anticipate what types of errors will occur or how to train to prevent them.

SUPERVISORY CONTROL IN DIFFERENT APPLICATIONS

This section, adapted from Sheridan (1982), provides brief comparisons and contrasts among different applications of supervisory control systems: process control, vehicle control, and manipulators.

Process Control

The term *process* usually refers to a dynamic system, such as a fossil fuel or nuclear power generating plant or a chemical or oil production facility, that is fixed in space and operates more or less continuously in time. Typically time constants are slow—many minutes or hours may elapse after a control action is taken before most of the system response is complete.

Most such processes involve large structures with fluids flowing from one place to another and involve the use of heat energy to affect the fluid or vice versa. Typically such systems involve multiple personnel and multiple machines, and at least some of the people move from one location of the process to another. Usually there is a central control room where many measured signals are displayed and where valves, pumps, and other devices are controlled.

Supervisory control has been emerging as an element in process control for several decades. Starting with electromechanical controllers or control stations that could be adjusted by the operator to maintain certain variables within limits (a home thermostat is an example), special electronic circuits gradually replaced the electromechanical function. In such systems the operator can become part of the control loop by switching to manual control. Usually each control station displays both the variable being controlled (e.g., room temperature for the thermostat) and the control signal (e.g., the flow of heat from the furnace). Many such manual control devices may be lined up in the control room, together with manual switches and valves, status lights, dials and recording displays, and as many as 1,500 alarms or annunciators--windows that light up to indicate what plant variable has just gone above or below limits. From the pattern of these alarms (e.g., 500 in the first minute of a loss-of-coolant accident and 800 in the second minute, by recent count, in a large new nuclear plant) the operator is supposed to divine what is happening.

The large, general-purpose computer has found its way into process control. Instead of multiple, independent, conventional proportional-integral-derivative controllers for each variable, the computer can treat the set of variables as a vector and compute the control trajectory that would be optimal (in the sense of quickest, most efficient, or whatever criterion is important). Because there are many more interactions than the number of variables, the variety of displayed signals and the number of possible adjustments or programs the human operator may input to the computer-controller are potentially much greater than before. Thus there is now a great need, accelerated since the events at Three Mile Island, to develop displays that integrate complex patterns of information and allow the operator to issue commands in a natural, efficient, and reliable manner. The term <u>system state vector</u> is a fashionable way to describe the display of minimal chunks of information (using G. A. Miller's well-known terminology) to convey more meaning about the current state vector of variables, where it has been in the past, and where it is likely to go in the near future.

Vehicle Control

Unlike the processes described above, vehicles move through space and carry their operators with them or are controlled remotely. Various types of vehicles have come under a significant degree of supervisory control in the last 30 years.

We might start with spacecraft because, in a sense, their function is the simplest. They are launched to perform well-defined missions, and their interaction with their environment (other than gravity) is nil. In other words, there are no obstacles and no unpredictable traffic to worry about. It was in spacecraft, especially Apollo, that human operators who were highly skilled at continuous manual control (test pilots or "joy stick jockeys") had to adapt to a completely new way of getting information from the vehicle and giving it commands—this new way was to program the computer. The astronauts had to learn to use a simple keyboard with programs (different functions appropriate to different mission phases), nouns (operands, or data to be addressed or processed) and verbs (operations, or actions to be performed on the nouns).

Of course, the astronauts still performed a certain number of continuous control functions. They controlled the orientation of the vehicle and maneuvered it to accomplish star sighting, thrust, rendezvous, and lunar landing. But, as is not generally appreciated by the public, control in each of these modes was heavily aided. Not only were the manual control loops themselves stabilized by electronics, but also nonmanual, automatic control functions were being simultaneously executed and coordinated with what the astronauts did.

In commercial and military aircraft there has been more and more supervisory control in the last decade or two. Commercial pilots are called __flight managers__, indicative of the fact that they must allocate their attention among a large number of separate but complex computer-based systems. Military aircraft are called __flying computers__, and indeed the cost of the electronics in them now far exceeds the cost of the basic airframe. By means of inertial measurement, a feature of the new jumbo jets as well as of military aircraft, the computer can take a vehicle to any latitude, longitude, and altitude within a fraction of a kilometer. In addition there are many other supervisory command modes intermediate between such high-level commands and the lowest level of pure continuous control of ailerons, elevators, and thrust. A pilot can set the autopilot to provide a display of a smooth command course at fixed turn or climb rates to follow manually or can have the vehicle slaved to this course. The autopilot can be set to achieve a new altitude on a new heading. The pilot can lock onto radio beams or radar signals for automatic landing. In the Lockheed L-1011, for example, there are at least 10 separate identifiable levels of control. It is important for the pilot to have reliable means of breaking out of these automatic control modes and reverting to manual control or some intermediate mode. For example, when in an automatic landing mode the pilot can either push a yellow button on the control yoke or jerk the yoke back to manually get the aircraft back under direct control.

Air traffic control poses interesting supervisory control problems, for the headways (spacing) between aircraft in the vicinity of major commercial airports are getting tighter and tighter, and efforts both to save fuel and to avoid noise over densely populated urban areas require more radical takeoff and landing trajectories. New computer-based communication aids will supplement purely verbal communication between pilots and ground controllers, and new display technology will help the already overloaded ground controllers monitor what is happening in three-dimensional space over larger areas, providing predictions of collision and related vital information. The CDTI (cockpit display of traffic information) is a new computer-based picture of weather, terrain hazards such as mountains and tall structures, course information such as way points, radio beacons and markers, and runways and command flight patterns as well as the position, altitude, heading (and even predicted position) of other aircraft. It makes the pilot less dependent on ground control, especially when out-the-window visibility is poor.

More recently ships and submarines have been converting to supervisory control. Direct manual control by experienced helmsmen, which sufficed for many years, has been replaced both by the installation of inertial navigation, which calls for computer control and provides capability never before available, and by the trends toward higher speed and long time lags produced by larger size (e.g., the new supertankers). New autopilots and computer-based display aids, similar to those in aircraft, are now being used in ships.

Manipulators and Discrete Parts Handling

In a sense, manipulators combine the functions of process control and vehicle control. The manipulator base may be carried on a spacecraft, a ground vehicle, or a submarine, or its base may be fixed. The hand (gripper, end effector) is moved relative to the base in up to three degrees of translation and three degrees of rotation. It may have one degree of freedom for gripping, but some hands have differentially movable fingers or otherwise have more degrees of freedom to perform special cutting, drilling, finishing, cleaning, welding, paint spraying, sensing, or other functions.

Manipulators are being used in many different applications, including lunar moving vehicles, undersea operations, and hazardous operations in industry. The type of supervisory control and its justification differs according to the application.

The fact of a three-second time delay in the earth-lunar control loop resulting from round-trip radio transmission from earth leads to instabilities, unless an operator waits three seconds after each of a series of incremental movements. This makes direct manual control time-consuming and impractical. Sheridan and Ferrell (1967) proposed having a computer on the moon receive commands to complete segments of a movement task locally using local sensors and local computer program control. They proposed calling this mode supervisory control. Delays in sending the task segments from earth to moon would be unimportant, so long as rapid local control could introduce actions to deal with obstacles or other self-protection rapidly.

The importance of supervisory control to the undersea vehicle manipulator is also compelling. There are things the operator cannot sense or can sense only with great difficulty and time delay (e.g., the mud may easily be stirred up, producing turbid opaque water that prevents the video camera from seeing), so that local sensing and quick response may be more reliable. For monotonous tasks (e.g., inspecting pipelines, structures, or ship hulls or surveying the ocean bottom to find some object) the operator cannot remain alert for long; if adequate artificial sensors could be provided for the key variables, supervisory control should be much more reliable. The human operator may have other things to do, so that supervisory control would facilitate periodic checks to update the computer program or help the remote device get out of trouble. A final reason for supervisory control, and often the most acceptable, is that, if communications, power, or other systems fail, there are fail-safe control modes into which the remote system reverts to get the vehicle back to the surface or otehwise render it recoverable.

Many of these same reasons for supervisory control apply to other uses of manipulators. Probably the greatest current interest in manipulators is for manufacturing (so-called industrial robots), including machining, welding, paint spraying, heat treatment, surface cleaning, bin picking, parts feeding for punch presses, handling between transfer lines, assembly, inspection, loading and unloading finished units, and warehousing. Today repetitive tasks such as welding and paint spraying can be programmed by the supervisor, then implemented with the control loops that report position and velocity. If the parts conveyor is sufficiently reliable, welding or painting nonexistent objects seldom occurs, so that more sophisticated feedback, involving touch or vision, is usually not required. Manufacturing assembly, however, has proven to be a far more difficult task.

In contrast to assembly line operations, in which, even if there is a mix of products, every task is prespecified, in many new applications of manipulators with supervisory control, each new task is unpredictable to considerable extent. Some examples are mining, earth moving, building construction, building and street cleaning and maintenance, trash collection, logging, and crop harvesting, in which large forces and power must be applied to external objects. The human operator is necessary to program or otherwise guide the manipulator in some degrees of freedom, to accomodate each new situation; in other respects certain characteristic motions are preprogrammed and need only to be initiated at the correct time. In some medical applications, such as microsurgery, the goal is to minify rather than enlarge motions and forces, to extend the surgeon's hand tools through tiny body cavities to cut, to obtain tissue samples, to remove unhealthy tissue, or to stitch. Again, the surgeon controls some degrees of freedom (e.g., of an optical probe or a cauterizing snare), while automation controls other variables (e.g., air or water pressure).

THEORY AND METHOD

There are a number of limited theories and methods in the human factors literature that should be brought to bear on the use of supervisory control systems. A great deal remains to be done, however, to apply them in this context. The discussion that follows deals with five aspects of the problem. The first considers current formal models of supervisory control. The second discusses display and command problems. The third takes up computer knowledge-based systems and their relation to the internal cognitive model of the operator for on-line decision making in supervisory control. The fourth deals with mental workload, stress, and research on attention and resource allocation as they relate to supervisory control. The fifth is concerned with issues of human error, system reliability, trust, and ultimate authority.

Modeling Supervisory Control

In the area of real-time monitoring and control of continuous dynamic processes, the optimal control model (Baron and Kleinman, 1969) describes the perceptual motor behavior of closed-loop systems having relatively short time constants. Experimentation on this topic has been limited, suggesting that this class of model may be broadened to represent monitoring and discrete decision behavior in dynamic systems in which control is infrequent (Levison and Tanner, 1971). There are also attempts to extend this work to explore its applicability to more complex systems (Baron, et al., 1981; Kok and Stassen, 1980).

An increasing number of supervisory control systems can be represented by a hierarchy of three kinds of interaction (Sheridan, 1982): (1) a human operator interacting with a high-level computer, (2) low-level computers interacting with physical entities in the environment, and (3) the resulting multilevel and multi-loop interaction, having interesting symmetrical properties (Figure 4-1). Since there are three levels of intelligence (one human, two artificial), the allocation of cognitive and computational tasks among the three becomes central. Using Rasmussen's (1979) categorization of behavior into knowledge-based, rule-based, and skill-based behavior, the operator may assign rule-based tasks (e.g., pattern recognition, running planning and predictive models, organizing) to the high-level computer (Figure 4-2). Similarly, skill-based tasks (filtering, display generation, servo-control) may be assigned to various low-level computers. The operator must concentrate on the environmental tasks that compete for his attention, allocating his attention among five roles: (1) planning what to do next, (2) teaching or on-line programming of the computer(s), (3) monitoring the (semi)

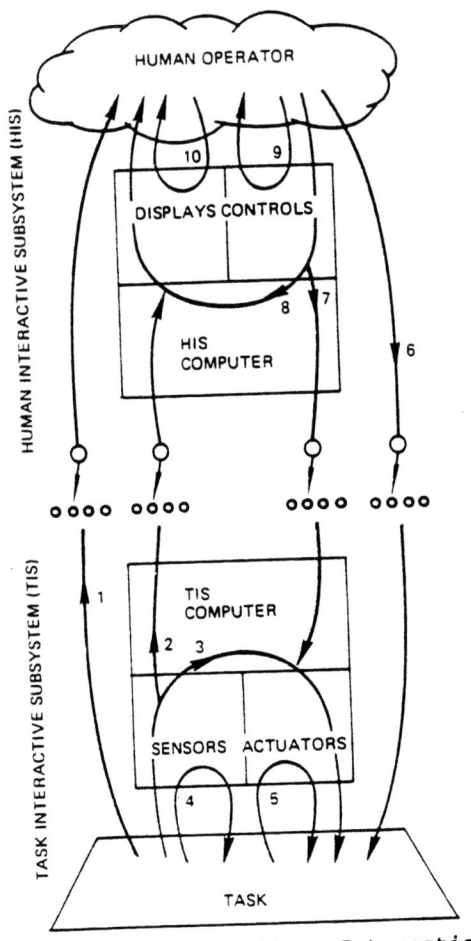

FIGURE 4-1 Multiloop Interaction in a Supervisory Control System

1. Task is observed directly by human operator.
2. Task is observed indirectly through sensors, computers, and displays. This TIS feedback interacts with HIS feedback.
3. Task is controlled within TIS automatic mode.
4. Task is affected by the process of being sensed.
5. Task affects actuators and in turn is affected.
6. Human operator directly affects task.
7. Human operator affects task indirectly through controls, HIS computers, and actuators. This control interacts with that from TIS.
8. Human operator gets feedback from HIS.
9. Human operator adjusts control parameters.
10. Human operator adjusts display parameters.

automatic behavior of the system for abnormalities, (4) intervening when necessary to make adjustments, maintaining, repairing, or assuming direct control, and (5) learning from experience.

Display and Command

Design of integrated computer-generated displays is not a new problem, and the military services and space agencies

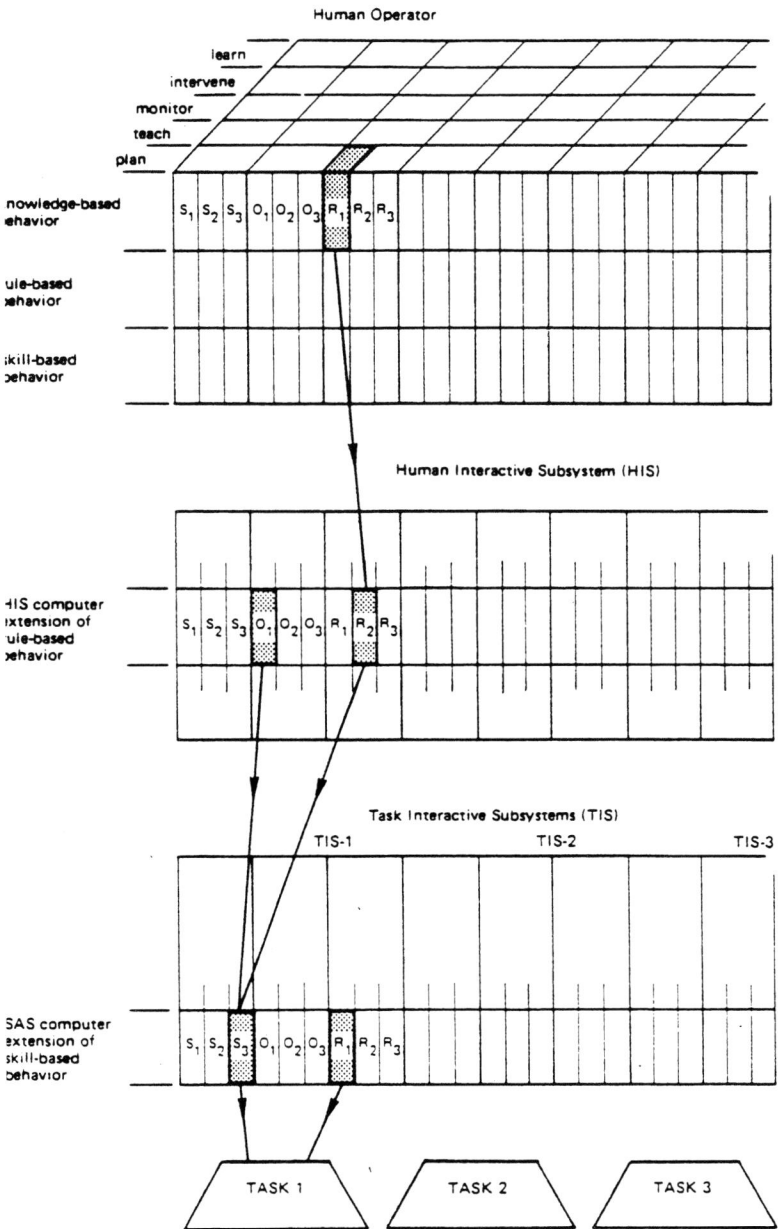

FIGURE 4-2 Multilevel Allocation of Tasks in a Supervisory Control System

have pioneered developments in this area for aircraft and various command and control systems. But the technology continues to create more possibilities. Operators of supervisory control systems need to have fewer displays, not more, telling them what they want or need to know when they want or need to know it. An additional design problem is that what operators think they need and what they really need may differ.

As computer collaborators become more and more sophisticated a useful type of display would tell the operator what the computer knows and assumes, both about the system and about the operator, and what it intends to do.

An important source of guidance regarding the design of displays has been and will continue to be the intuitive beliefs of experienced operators. The designer needs to know how much credence to give to these intuitions. Too little attention may mean forfeiting a valuable source of information; too much may result in inappropriate designs that fit untested folk wisdom (a pilot's belief in the value of verisimilitude in displays is an example of the latter problem). Ericsson and Simon's taxonomy (1980) of situations in which introspection is more and less valid is one point of departure for research. Studies of metacognition, people's understanding of their own cognitive processes (as contrasted with current psychological understanding), are a second (Cavanaugh and Borkowski, 1980). The studies of clinical judgment conducted in the 1950s and 1960s (Goldberg, 1968) are a third. These studies found that in the course of their diagnoses expert clinicians imagine that they rely on more variables and use them in more complex manner than appears to be the case from attempts to model their diagnostic processes.

Although good-quality computer-generated speech is both available and cheap, and although it can give operators warnings and other information without their prior attention being directed to it, little imaginative use of such a capability has been made as yet in supervisory control.

The use of command language has arisen more recently in conjunction with teaching or programming robot systems. A more primitive form of it is found in the new autopilot command systems in aircraft. Giving commands to a control system by means of strings of symbols in syntax is a new game for most operators. Progress in this area depends on careful technology transfer from data processing that is self-paced to dynamic control in which the pace is determined by many factors. Naturalness in use of such language is also an important goal.

Command, in many circumstances, is not a solitary task. The operator must interact with many individuals in order to get a job done. This may be particularly the case when the nature of the emergency means that the technical system cannot be trusted to report and respond reliably--that is, an interacting human system may assume (and perhaps interface with) some of the functions of the interacting technical system. The kinds of human interaction possible include requesting information, monitoring the response of the system, notifying outsiders (e.g., for evacuation, to provide special skills), and terminating unnecessary communications. When are these interactions initiated? How valid are the cues? What features of technical systems make such intervention more and less feasible? How does having others around affect operators' thoughts and actions (e.g., are they more creative, more risk-averse, more careful)?

Another question that arises with multiperson systems is whether one individual (or group) should both monitor for and cope with crises. In medicine it is not always assumed that the same individual has expertise in both diagnosis and treatment. Perhaps in supervisory control systems the equivalent functions should be separated, and different training and temperament called for in monitoring and in intervention.

Computer Knowledge-Based Systems and the Operator's Internal Cognitive Model

It is not a new idea that, in performing a task, people somehow represent the task in their heads and calculate whether, given certain constraints, doing *this* will result in *that*. Such ideas derive from antiquity.

Human-Machine Control

In the 1950s the development of the "observer" in control systems theory formalized this idea. That is, a differential equation model of the external controlled process is included in the automatic controller and is driven by the same input that drives the actual process. Any discrepancy between the output of this computerized model of the environmental process and the actual process is fed back as a correction to the internal model to force its variables to be continuously the same as the actual process. Then any and all state variables as represented (observed) in the internal model may be used to directly control the process, if direct measurement of those same variables in the actual environment may be costly, difficult, or impossible. This physical realization of the traditional idea of the internal model probably provoked much of the current research in cognitive science.

Running in fast-time, updating initial conditions at each of a succession of such calculations, the model becomes a "predictor display" that provides the operator with a projection of what will happen under given assumptions of input (Kelly, 1968). Further comparisons can be made between outputs of such real-time models run in the computer and those of the operator's own internal model, not only for control but also for failure detection and isolation (Sheridan, 1981). Tsach has developed a realization of this as an operator aid for application to process control (Tsach et al., 1982).

Ideally the computer should keep the operator informed of what it is assuming and computing, and the operator should keep the computer informed of what he or she is thinking.

Cognitive Science

In the last several years cognitive psychology has contributed some theories about human inference that make the application of knowledge-based systems particularly relevant to supervisory control. The idea is that reasoning and decision making consist of the developing and searching of complex problem spaces (Newell and Simon, 1972) and of applying one or more inference procedures about information in a knowledge base that represents the decision maker's understanding of the situation (Collins and Loftus, 1975). This is similar to but more inclusive and less well developed than the internal process model used by control theorists. Rasmussen's (1979) qualitative model of human decision making about process control is entirely compatible with this view. And, the contribution of specialists in artificial intelligence concerning knowledge-based systems provides one way to implement the computer portion of such human-computer interaction.

A number of human factors problems relate to people's ability to hold in mind the basic workings of a complex system and to update that view depending on the current state of the system. Recent studies of cognitive processes in skilled operators such as taxi drivers (Chi et al., 1980) or chess players (Chase and Simon, 1973) begin to provide the kind of information that will be needed by human factors designers evaluating these issues. For example, how can people best be trained to develop effective problem spaces? What is the optimal mix of analog and digital representation? How can the computer's data base system be used to aid the individual in developing and updating of such an internal model? What means can be used to ensure that the current state of the model fits with the current state of the system? With what frequency should a person be interrogated about his or her current view of the model to make sure that he or she is still "with it" in control of the system? For human supervision to be really effective, a detailed understanding of how the human controller grasps a complex system at any moment in time and updates it over time is necessary.

How can we determine a given operator's internal cognitive model of a given task at a given time? One method is to ask the operator to express it in natural language, but the obvious difficulty is that each operator's expression is unique, making it very difficult to measure either discrepancy from reality or to compare across operators. Verbal protocol techniques (Bainbridge, 1974) make use of key words and relations. More formal psychometric techniques (multiattribute utility assessment, conjoint or multidimensional scaling, interpretive structural modeling, policy capturing, and fuzzy set theory) offer some promising ways of telling a computer one's knowledge and values in structural form.

A likely (and perhaps common) source of difficulty is a mismatch in the mental models of a system of those who design it and those who operate it. Operators who fail to recognize this disparity are subject to unpleasant surprises when the system behaves in unexpected ways. Operators who do recognize it may fail to exploit the full potential of the system for fear of surprises if they push it into unfamiliar territory (Young, 1981). On a descriptive level, it would be useful to understand the correspondence between the mental models of designers and operators as well as to know which experiences signal operators that there is a mismatch and how they cope with that information. On a practical level, it would be useful to know more about the possibility of improving the match of these two models by steps such as involving operators more in the design process or showing them how the design evolved (rather than giving them a reconstruction of its final state). The magnitude of these problems is likely to grow to the extent that designers and operators have different training, experience, and intensity of involvement with systems.

Mental Workload

The concept of mental workload as discussed in this section is not unique to supervisory control, but it is sufficiently important in this context to be included here as a special consideration.

Human-Machine Control (This section is adapted from Sheridan and Young, 1982).

During the last decade "mental workload" has become a concept of great controversy, not because of disagreement over whether it is important, but because of disagreement over how to define and measure it. Military specifications for mental workload are nevertheless being prepared by the Air Force, based on the assumption that mental workload measures will predict--either at the design stage or during a flight or other operation--whether an operation can succeed. In other words, it is believed that measurements of mental workload are more sensitive in anticipating when pilot or operator performance will break down than are conventional performance measures of the human-machine system.

At the present time "mental workload" is a construct. It must be inferred; it cannot be observed directly like human control response or system performance, although it might be defined operationally in terms of one or several or a battery of tests. There is a clear distinction between mental and physical workload: The latter is the rate of doing mechanical work and expending calories. There is consensus on measurements based on respiratory gases and other techniques for measuring physical workload.

Of particular concern are situations having sustained mental workloads of long duration. Many aircraft missions continue to require such effort by the crew. But the introduction of computers and automation in many systems has come to mean that for long periods of time operators have nothing to do--the workload may be so low as to result in boredom and serious decrement in alertness. The operator may then suddenly be expected to observe events on a display and make critical judgments--indeed, even to detect an abnormality, diagnose what failed, and take over control from the automatic system. One concern is that the operator, not being "in the loop," will not have kept up with what is going on, and will need time to reacquire that knowledge and orientation to make the proper diagnoses or take over control. Also of concern is that at the beginning of the transient the computer-based information will be opaque to the operator, and it will take some time even to figure out how to access and retrieve from the system the needed information.

There have been three approaches to measuring mental workload. One approach, used by the aircraft manufacturers, avoids coping directly with measurements of the operator per se and bases workload on a task time-line analysis: the more tasks the operator has to do per unit of time, the greater the workload. This provides a relative index of workload that characterizes task demand, other factors being equal. It says nothing about the mental workload of any actual person and indeed could apply to a task performed by a robot.

The second approach is perhaps the simplest--to use the operator's subjective ratings of his or her perceived mental workload. This may be done during or after the events judged. One form of this is a single-category scale similar to the Cooper-Harper scale for rating aircraft handling quality. Perhaps more interesting is a three-attribute scale, there being some consensus that "fraction of total time busy," "cognitive complexity," and "emotional stress" are rather different characteristics of mental workload and that one or two of these can be large when the other(s) are small. These scales have been used by the military services as well as aircraft manufacturers. A criticism of them is that people are not always good judges of their own ability to perform in the future. Some pilots may judge themselves to be quite capable of further sustained effort at a higher level when in fact they are not.

The third approach is the so-called secondary task or reserve capacity technique. In it a pilot or operator is asked to allocate whatever attention is left over from the primary task to some secondary task, such as verbally generating random numbers, tracking a dot on a screen with a small joy stick, etc. Theoretically, the better the performance on the secondary task, the less the time required and therefore the less the mental workload of the primary task. A criticism of this technique is that it is intrusive; it may itself reduce the attention allocated to the primary task and therefore be a self-contaminating measure. And, in real flight operations the crew may not be so cooperative in performing secondary tasks.

The fourth and final technique is really a whole category of partially explored possibilities--the use of physiological measures. Many such measures have been proposed, including changes in the electroencephalogram (ongoing or steady-state), evoked response potentials (the best candidate is the attenuation and latency of the so-called P_{300}, occurring 300 milliseconds after the onset of a challenging stimulus), heart rate variability, galvanic skin response, pupillary diameter, and frequency spectrum of the voice. All of these have proved to be noisy and unreliable.

Both the Air Force and the Federal Aviation Administration currently have major programs to develop workload measurement techniques for aircraft piloting and traffic control.

If an operator's mental workload appears to be excessive, there are several avenues for reducing it or compensating for it. First, one should examine the situation for causal factors that could be redesigned to be quicker, easier, or less anxiety-producing. Or perhaps parts of the task could be reassigned to others who are less loaded, or the procedure could be altered so as to stretch out in time the succession of events loading the particular operator. Finally, it may be possible to give all or part of the task to a computer or automatic system.

Cognitive Science

It is important, for purposes of evaluating both mental workload and cognitive models as discussed in the previous section, to note that there has been an enormous change in models of mental processing in both psychology and computer science. In their recent paper, Feldman and Ballard (in press) argue that:

> Contemporary computer science has sharpened our notions of what is "computable" to include bounds on time, storage and other resources. It does not

seem unreasonable to require that computational models and cognitive science be at least as plausible in their postulated resource requirement.

The critical resource that is most obvious is time. Neurons, whose basic computational speed is a few milliseconds must be made to account for complex behaviors which are carried out in a few hundred milliseconds . . . (Posner, 1978). This means that higher complex behaviors are carried out in less than a hundred time steps. It may appear that the problem posed here is inherently unsolvable and that we have made an error in our formulation, but recent results in computational complexity theory suggest that networks of active computing elements can carry out at least simple computations in the required time range—these solutions involve using massive numbers of units and connections and we also address the question of limitations on these resources.

There is also evidence from experimental psychology (Posner, 1978) that the human mind is, at least in part, a parallel system. From neuropsychological considerations there is reason to suppose that a parallelism is represented in regional areas of the brain responsible for different sorts of cognitive functions. For example, we know that different visual maps (Cowey, 1979) underlie object recognition and that separate portions of the cortex are involved in the comprehension and production of language. We also know more about the role of subcortical and cortical structures in motor control.

The study of mental workload has simply not kept up with these advances in the conceptualization of the human mind as a complex of subsystems. The majority of researchers of human workload have studied the interference of one complex task with another. There is abundant evidence in the literature that such interference does occur. However, this general interference may account for only a small part of the variance in total workload. More important may be the effects of the specific cognitive systems shared by two tasks. Indeed, Kinsbourne and Hicks (1978) have recently formulated a theory of attention in which the degree of facilitation or interference between tasks depends on the distance between their cortical representation. The notion of distance may be merely metaphorical, since we do not know whether it represents the actual physical distance on the cortex or whether it involves a relative interconnectivity of cortical area; the latter idea seems more reasonable.

Viewing humans in terms of cognitive subsystems changes the perspective on mental workload (see Navon and Gopher, 1979). It is unusual for any human task to involve only a single cognitive system or to occur at any fixed location in the brain. Most tasks differ in sensory modality, in central analysis systems, and in motor output systems. There is need for basic research to understand more about the separability and coordination of such cognitive systems. We also need a task analysis that takes advantage of the new cognitive systems approach to ask how tasks distribute themselves among different cognitive systems and when performance of different tasks may draw on the same cognitive system. There is also an obvious connection between a cognitive systems approach and analysis of individual differences based on psychometric or information processing concepts, and much needs to be done to link analysis of individual abilities to the ability to time-share activity within the same cognitive system or across different systems (Landman and Hunt, 1982).

An emphasis on separable cognitive systems does not necessarily mean that a more unified central controlling system is unnecessary. Indeed, widespread interference between tasks of very different types (Posner, 1980) suggests that such a central controller is a necessary aspect of human performance. There are a number of theoretical views addressing the problem of self-regulation of behavior, particularly in stressful situations. Two principles have been applied by human factors engineers: The first is that attention narrows under stress. Thus, more attention is allocated to central aspects of the task while less attention is allocated to more peripheral or secondary aspects. Sometimes this principle has been applied to positions in visual space, arguing that peripheral vision is sacrified more than central vision under stress. The degree to which the general principle applies automatically to positions in visual space or to allocation of function within tasks is simply not very well understood--but it should be. A second principle of the relationship between stress and attention suggests that under stress habitual behaviors take precedence over new or novel behaviors. The idea is that behaviors originally learned under stressful conditions tend to return when conditions are again stressful. This view is particularly important with respect to the process of changing people from one task layout to another. If the original learning takes place under high stress conditions while transition occurs under relatively low stress conditions, a stressful situation may tend to reinstate the responses learned in the original configuration.

Recently cognitive psychologists have begun to take into account emotional responses produced under conditions of stress (Bower, 1981). One development emphasizes links between individual differences in emotional responding and attention (see Posner and Rothbart, 1980, for a review). Although it is a highly speculative hypothesis at this time, this work suggests that attention may be viewed as a method for controlling the degree of emotional responding that occurs during stressful conditions. In particular, differences in personality and temperament may affect the degree to which attention and other mechanisms are successful in managing stress. These new models relate emotional responding to more cognitive processes. They have the potential of helping us understand more about the effects of emotion and how it may guide cognition and behavior under stressful conditions. Since this work has just begun, there are few general principles to link the emotional responses to cognition as yet. Developments along this line could be useful for human factors engineers, particularly those involved in training and retraining and those involved in mangement of stress under battlefield conditions.

For the most part, this discussion has been from the viewpoint of the overloaded operator. For much of the time, however, the operator may be underloaded. In the field of vigilance research, which is concerned with human behavior in systems in which signal detection is required but the signals are infrequent and difficult to detect, a great deal is known about exactly what parameters of signal presentation affect performance. The signal detection model (Green and Swets, 1966) has been shown to be useful in analyzing such behavior. Again, its applicability has not been evaluated in more complex tasks in which signals are represented by more complex patterns of activity as would be the case in supervisory control systems of the types described above.

Human Proficiency and Error: Culpability, Trust, and Ultimate Authority

Designers of the large, complex, capital-intensive, high-risk-of-failure systems we have been discussing would like to automate human operators out of their systems. But they know they must depend on them to plan, program, monitor, step in when failures occur with the automation, and generalize on system experience. They are also terrified of human error.

Both the commercial aviation and the nuclear power industries are actively collecting data on human error and trying to use it analytically in conjunction with data on failures in physical components and subsystems to predict the reliability of overall systems. The public and the Congress, in a sense, are demanding it, on the assumption that it is clear what human error is, how to measure it, and even how to stop it.

Human error is commonly thought of as a mistake of action or judgment that could have been avoided had the individual been more alert, attentive, or conscientious. That is, the source of error is considered to be internal and therefore within the control of the individual and not induced by external factors such as the design of the equipment, the task requirements, or lack of adaquate training.

Some behavioral scientists may claim that people err because they are operating "open loop"--without adequate feedback to tell them when they are in error. They would have supervisory control systems designers provide feedback at every potential misstep. Product liability litigants sometimes take a more extreme stance--that equipment should be designed so that it is error proof, without the opportunity for people to (begin to) err, get feedback, then correct themselves.

The concept of human error needs to be examined. The assertion that an error has been committed implies a sharp and agreed-upon dividing line between right and wrong, a simple binary classification that is obviously an oversimplification. Human decision and action involve a multidimensional continuum of perceiving, remembering, planning, even socially interacting. Clearly the fraction of errors in any set of human response data is a function of where the boundry is drawn. How does one decide where to draw the line dividing right from wrong across the many dimensions of behavior? In addition, is an error of commission, (e.g., actuating a switch when it is not expected), equivalent to an error of omission, (e.g., failing to actuate a switch when it is expected)? Is it useful to say, in both these instances, an error has been <u>committed</u>? What then exactly do we mean by human error?

People tend to differ from machines in that people are more inclined to make "common-mode errors," in which one failure leads to another, presumably because of concurrency of stimuli or responses in space or time. Furthermore, as suggested earlier, if a person is well practiced in a procedure ABC, and must occassionally do DBE, he or she is quite likely in the latter case to find himself or herself doing DBC. This type of error is well documented in process control, in which many and varied procedures are followed. In addition, when people are under stress of emergency they tend more often to err (sometimes, however, analysts may assume that operators are aware of an emergency when they are not). People are also able to discover and correct their own errors, which they surely do in many large-scale systems to avert costly accidents.

Presumably the rationale for defining human error is to develop means for predicting when they are likely to occur and for reducing their frequency (Swain and Gutman, 1980). Various taxonomies of human error have been devised. There are errors of omission and errors of comission. Errors may be associated with sensing, memory, decision making, or motor skill. Norman (1981) distinguishes mistakes (wrong intention) from slips (correct intention but wrong action). But at present there is no accepted taxonomy on which to base the definition of human error, nor is there agreement on the dimensions of behavior that should be invoked in such a taxonomy.

There is usefulness in both a case study approach to human error and in the accumulation of statistics on errors that lead to accidents. Both these approaches, however, require that the investigator have a theory or model of human error or accident causation and the framework from which to approach the analysis. In addition there is a need to understand the causal chain between human error and accident.

One has only to examine a sampling of currently used accident reporting forms to realize the importance of the need for a framework for analyzing human error. They range from medical history forms to equipment failure reports. None that we have examined deals satisfactorily with the role of human behavior in contributing to the accident circumstances.

Furthermore, for accident reports to be useful, their aim needs to be specified. There is an inherent conflict between the goals of understanding what happened and attempting to fix blame for it. The former requires candor, whereas the latter discourages it. Other potential biases in these reports include: (a) exaggerating in hindsight what could have been anticipated in foresight; (b) being unable to reconstruct or retrieve hypotheses about what was happening that no longer makes sense in retrospect; (c) telescoping the sequence of events (making their temporal course seem shorter and more direct); (d) exaggerating one's own role in events; (e) failing to see the internal logic of others' actions (from their own perspective). Variants of these reporting biases have been observed elsewhere (Nisbett and Ross, 1980). Their presence and virulence in accident reports on supervisory control systems merits attention.

In addition to these fundamental research needs, there is a variety of related issues particularly relevant to supervisory control systems that should be addressed.

In supervisory control systems it is becoming more and more difficult to establish blame, for the information exchange between operators and computers is complex, and the "error," if there ever was any, could be in hardware or software design, maintenance, or management.

Most of us think we observe that people are better at some kinds of tasks than computers, and computers are better at some others. Therefore, it seems that it would be quite clear how roles should be allocated between people and computers. But the interactions are often so subtle as to elude understanding. It is also conventional wisdom to say that people should have the ultimate authority over machines. But again, in actual operating systems we usually find ourselves ill prepared to assert which should have authority under what circumstances and for how long.

Operators in such systems usually receive fairly elaborate training in both theory and operating skills. The latter is or should be done on simulators, since in actual systems the most important (critical) events for which the operator needs training seldom occur. Unfortunately there has been a tendency to standardize the emergencies (classic stall or engine fire in aircraft, large-break loss-of-cooling accident in nuclear plants) and repeat them on the simulator until they become fixed patterns of response. There seldom is emphasis on responding to new, unusual emergencies, failures in combination, etc., which the rule book never anticipated. Simulators would be especially good for such training.

A frustrating, and perhaps paradoxical, feature of "emergency" intervention is that supervisors must still rely on and work with systems that they do not entirely trust. The nature and success of their intervention is likely to depend on their appraisal of which aspects of the system are still reliable. Research might help predict what doubts about related malfunctions are and are not aroused by a particular malfunction. Does the spread of suspicion follow the operator's mental model (e.g., lead to other mechanically connected subsystems) or along a more associative line (e.g., mistrust all dials)? A related problem is how experience with one malfunction of a complex system cues the interpretation of subsequent malfunctions. Is the threshold of mistrust lowered? Is there an unjustified assumption that the same problem is repeating itself, or that the same information-searching procedures are needed? How is the expectation of successful coping affected? Do operators assume that they will have the same amount of time to diagnose and act? Finally, how does that experience generalize to other technical systems? Do bad experiences lead to a general resistance to innovation?

A key to answering these questions is understanding the operators' own attribution processes. Do they subscribe to the same definition of human error as do those who evaluate their performance? What gives them a feeling of control? How do they assign responsibility for successful and unsuccessful experiences? Although their mental models should provide some answers to these questions, others may be sought in general principles of causal attribution and misattribution (Harvey, et al., 1976).

CONCLUSIONS AND RECOMMENDATIONS

Supervisory control of large, complex, capital-intensive, high-risk systems is a general trend, driven both by new technology and by the belief that this mode of control will provide greater efficiency and reliability. The human factors aspects of supervisory control have been neglected. Without further research they may well become the bottleneck and most vulnerable or most sensitive aspect of these systems. Reseach is needed on:

(1) How to display integrated dynamic system relationships in a way that is understandable and accessible. This includes how best to allow the computer to tell the operator what it knows, assumes, and intends.

(2) How best to allow the operator to tell the computer what he or she wants and why, in a flexible and natural way.
(3) How to discover the internal cognitive model of the environmental process that the operator is controlling and improve that cognitive representation if it is inappropriate.
(4) How to aid the cognitive process by computer-based knowledge structures and planning models.
(5) Why people make errors in system operation, how to minimize these errors, and how to factor human errors into analyses of system reliability.
(6) How mental workload affects human error making in systems operation and refinement and standardization of definitions and measures of mental workload.
(7) Whether human operator or computer should have authority under what circumstances.
(8) How to coordinate the efforts of the different humans involved in supervisory control of the same system.
(9) How best to learn from experience with such large, complex, interactive systems.
(10) How to improve communication between the designers and operators of technical systems.

Research is needed to improve our understanding of human-computer collaboration in such systems and on how to characterize it in models. The validation of such models is also a key problem, not unlike the problem of validating socioeconomic or other large-scale system models.

In view of the scale of supervisory control systems, closer collaboration between researchers and systems designers in the development of such systems may be the best way for such research, modeling, and validation to occur. And perhaps data collection should be built in to the normal--and abnormal--operation of such systems.

REFERENCES

Bainbridge, L.
    1974   Analysis of verbal protocols from a process control task. In E. Edwards and F. Lees, eds., <u>The Human Operator in Process Control</u>. London: Taylor and Francis.

Baron, S., Zacharias, G., Muralidharan, R., and Lancraft, R.
   1981   PROCRU: A model for analyzing flight crew procedures in approach to landing. In Proceedings of the Eighth IFAC World Congress, Tokyo.

Baron, S., and Kleinman, D.
   1969   The human as an optimal controller and information processor. IEEE Trans. Man-Machine Systems MSS-10(11):9-17.

Bower, G.
   1981   Mood and memory. American Psychologist 36:129-148.

Cavanaugh, J. C., and Borkowski, J. G.
   1980   Searching for meta-memory-memory connections. Developmental Psychology 16:441-453.

Chase, W. G., and Simon, H. A.
   1973   The mind's eye in chess. In W. G. Chase, ed., Visual Information Processing. New York: Academic Press.

Chi, M. T. H., Chase, W. G., and Eastman, R.
   1980   Spatial Representation of Taxi Drivers. Paper presented to the Psychonomics Society, St. Louis, November.

Collis, A. M., and Loftus, E. M.
   1975   A spreading activation theory of semantic processing. Psychological Review 82:407-428.

Cowey, A.
   1979   Cortical maps and visual perception. Quarterly Journal of Experimental Psychology 31:1-17.

Ericsson, A., and Simon, H.
   1980   Verbal reports as data. Psychological Review 87:215-251.

Feldman, J. A., and Ballard, D. H.
   in press   Connectionist models and their properties. In J. Beck and A. Rosenfeld, eds., Human and Computer Vision. New York: Academic Press.

Goldberg, L. R.
   1968   Simple models or simple processes? Some research on clinical judgments. American Psychologist 23:483-496.

Green, D. M., and Swets, J. A.
   1966   Signal Detection Theory and Psychophysics. New York: John Wiley.

Harvey, J. H., Ickes, W. J., and Kidd, R. F., eds.
   1976   New Directions in Attribution Research. Hillsdale, N. J.: Lawrence Erlbaum.

Kelly, C.
  1968   Manual and Automatic Control. New York: John Wiley.

Kinsbourne, M., and Hicks, R. L.
  1978   Functional cerebral space: a model for overflow transfer and interference effects in human performance. In J. Requin, ed., Attention and Performance VIII. Hillsdale, N.J.: Lawrence Erlbaum.

Kok, J. J., and Stassen, H. G.
  1980   Human operator control of slowly responding systems: supervisory control. Journal of Cybernetics and Information Sciences 3:124-174.

Landman, M., and Hunt, E. B.
  1982   Individual differences in secondary task performance. Memory and Cognition 10:10-25.

Levison, W. H., and Tanner, R. B.
  1971   A Control-Theory Model for Human Decision Making. National Aeronautics and Space Administration CR-1953, December.

Navon, D., and Gopher, D.
  1979   On the economy of the human-processing system. Psychological Review 86:214-230.

Newell, A., and Simon, H. A.
  1972   Human Problem Solving. Englewood Cliffs, N. J.: Prentice-Hall.

Nisbett, R., and Ross, L.
  1980   Human Inference: Strategies and Shortcomings of Social Judgment. Englewood Cliffs, N. J.: Prentice-Hall.

Norman, D. A.
  1981   Categorization of action slips. Psychological Review 88:1-15.

Posner, M. I.
  1978   Chronometric Explorations of Mind. Hillsdale, N. J.: Lawrence Erlbaum.
  1980   Orienting of attention. Quarterly Journal of Experimental Psychology 32:3-25.

Posner, M. I., and Rothbart, M. K.
  1980   Development of attentional mechanisms. In J. Flowers, ed., Nebraska Symposium. Lincoln: University of Nebraska Press.

Rasmussen, J.
  1979   On the Structure of Knowledge--A Morphology of Mental Models in a Man-Machine System Context. RISO National Laboratory Report M-2192. Roskilde, Denmark.

Sheridan, T.
1981   Understanding human error and aiding human diagnostic behavior in nuclear power plants. In J. Rasmussen and W. Rouse, eds., *Human Detection and Diagnosis of System Failures*. New York: Plenum Press.
1982   Supervisory Control: Problems, Theory and Experiment in Application to Undersea Remote Control Systems. MIT Man-Machine Systems Laboratory Report. February.

Sheridan, T., and Ferrell, W. R.
1967   Supervisory control of manipulation. Pp. 315-323 in Proceedings of the 3rd Annual Conference on Manual Control. NASA SP-144.

Sheridan, T. B, and Young, L. R.
1982   Human Factors in aerospace. In R. Dehart, ed., *Fundamentals of Aerospace Medicine*. Philadelphia: Lea and Febiger.

Swain, A. D., and Guttman, H. E.
1980   *Handbook of Human Reliability Analysis with Emphasis on Nuclear Power Plant Applications* NUREG/CR 1278. Washington, D.C.: Nuclear Regulatory Commission.

Tsach, U., Sheridan, T. B., and Tzelgov, J.
in press   A New Method for Failure Detection and Location in Complex Systems. Proceedings of the 1982 American Control Conference. New York: Institute of Electrical and Electronics Engineers.

U.S. Army Research Institute
1979   *Annual Report on Research, 1979*. Alexandria, Va.: Army Research Institute for the Behavioral and Social Sciences.

Young, R. M.
1981   The machine inside the machine: users' models of pocket calculators. *International Journal of Man-Machine Studies* 15:51-85.

Zajonc, R. B.
1980   Feeling and knowledge: preferences need no inferences. *American Psychologist* 35:151-175.

5

USER-COMPUTER INTERACTION

INTRODUCTION

Electronic computers have probably had a more profound effect on our society, on our ways of living, and on our ways of doing business than any other technological creation of this century. Computers help manage our finances, checking accounts, and charge accounts. They help schedule rail and air travel, book theatre tickets, check out groceries, diagnose illnesses, teach our children, and amuse us with sophisticated games. Computers make it possible to erase time and distance through telecommunications, thereby giving us the freedom to choose the times and places at which we work. They help guide planes, direct missiles, guard our shores, and plan battle strategies. Computers have created new industries and have spawned new forms of crime. In reality, computers have become so intricately woven into the fabric of daily life that without them our civilization could not function as it does today. Small wonder that all these effects have been described as the results of a computer revolution.

Gantz and Peacock (1981) estimate that the total computer power available to U.S. businesses increased tenfold in the last decade, and that it is expected to double every two to four years. According to the most recently available estimates (U.S. Bureau of the Census, 1979), there are currently about 15 million computers, terminals, and electronic office machines in the United States. That number is expected to grow to about 30-35 million by 1985,

---

The principal authors of this chapter are Alphonse Chapanis, Nancy S. Anderson, and J. C. R. Licklider.

at which time there will be roughly one computer-based machine for every three persons employed in the white-collar work force. Spectacular advances in computer technology have made this growth possible, decreasing the cost of computer hardware at the rate of about 30 percent a year during the past few decades (Dertouzos and Moses, 1980).

Computers are still not as widely accepted as they might be. In a study by Zoltan and Chapanis (1982) on what professionals think about computers, over 500 certified public accountants, lawyers, pharmacists, and physicians in the Baltimore area filled out a 64-item questionnaire on their experiences with and attitudes toward electronic computers. Six factors emerged from a factor analysis of the data. Factor I, the largest in terms of the variance accounted for, is a highly positive grouping of adjectives attesting to the competence and productivity of computers, such as efficient, precise, reliable, dependable, effective, and fast. Factor II, the second largest in terms of the variance accounted for, is made up of highly negative adjectives: dehumanizing, depersonalizing, impersonal, cold, and unforgiving.

Still another factor in the Zoltan-Chapanis study indicates discontent with computers in terms of their ease of use. The respondents thought that computers are difficult and complicated and that computing languages are not simple to understand. These views are apparent in their responses to such statements as: "I would like a computer to accept ordinary English statements" and "I would like a computer to accept the jargon of my profession," both of which they agreed with strongly.

The findings of that study are generally in agreement with more informal reports in the popular press and other media about difficulties people have with computers and their use. Indeed, concerns about making computers easy to use can have serious economic consequences that may have to be faced by more and more computer manufacturers. For example, a small company in California was recently awarded a verdict for substantial monetary damages because of the inadequate performance of a computer that the company had purchased (Bigelow, 1981). In rendering his opinion substantiating the award, the presiding judge said, "It's a particularly serious problem, it seems to me, in the computer industry, particularly in that part of the industry which makes computers for first-time users, and seeks to expand the use of computers by . . .

targeting as purchasers businesses that have never used computers before, who don't have any experience in them, and who don't know what the consequences are of a defect and a failure" (Bigelow, 1981:94).

In Europe resistance to computerization has taken a somewhat different form than that in the United States. Television programs roughly equivalent to the American program __60 Minutes__ have been broadcast about the real and imagined evils of computers. Several countries--Austria, England, France, Germany, and Sweden among them--have prepared strict standards for the design of computer systems and have enacted federal laws restricting hours of work at computer terminals. Similar regulations may soon be in effect in this country. One difficulty is that current standards and regulations about computers are sometimes based on skimpy and unreliable data and sometimes on no data at all (Rupp, 1981). Whatever their origins, these events and trends are symptoms of fairly widespread uneasiness and malaise about computers, their usefulness, and usability. No one denies that computers are here to stay. The important question is: "How can we best design them for effective human use?" This chapter describes some of the research needed to answer that question.

Research needs are identified throughout the chapter. However desirable it might appear to assign specific priorities to each, we feel that it is difficult and risky to do so for at least three reasons. First, computer hardware, software, and interface design features are changing very rapidly (for a summary of the trends and progress in computer development see Branscomb, 1982). So, for example, the increased availability of modularly arranged components for microcomputers for personal use, in the office and at school as well as new networking and communications features allow design improvements to be made quickly by trial and error. As Nickerson (1969) has pointed out, such trial-and-error design improvements can be made more quickly than they could be by careful laboratory research studies.

Second, practical considerations are likely to be significant determinants of what research can be performed. Operational computer systems rarely can be disrupted for research purposes, and up-to-date hardware and software as well as appropriate groups of users are not always available. Under these circumstances it takes great ingenuity to conduct human factors research on user-computer interactions that can produce useful, generalizable results. Constraints and opportunities are therefore more likely than assigned priorities to dictate what research is performed.

Third, there is a definite need for good human factors research in all the areas we discuss, even with the caveat that technology is changing rapidly and good research is difficult to conduct. With these qualifications in mind, we do provide at certain places in this chapter, short summaries indicating those research needs that we feel have higher priorities than others.

THE COMPUTER SYSTEM

Computer systems and their environments have been diagrammed and modeled in various ways. Figure 5-1 illustrates elements that are important from a human factors standpoint: the user, the task, the hardware, the software, the procedures, and the work environment. Together they cluster around what is commonly called the user-computer interface--that invisible surface that binds the various elements together. Diagramming a computer system in this way is to a large extent artificial, because the various elements cannot really be considered in isolation. As will be apparent later on, there are interactions among all of them. The figure is merely a convenient way of

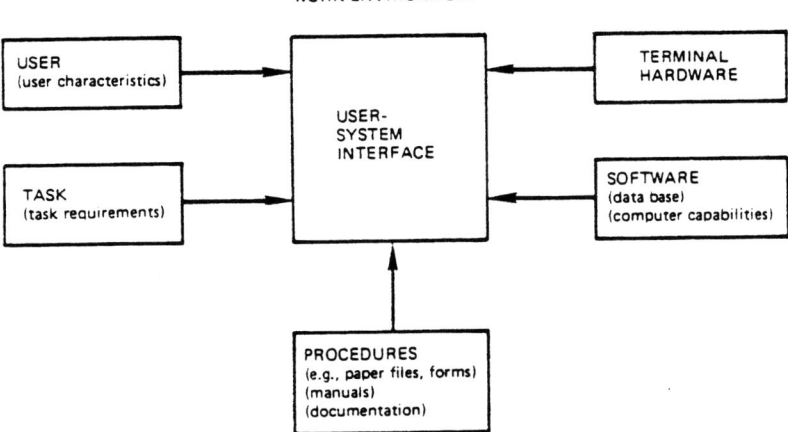

FIGURE 5-1   Important Elements of Computer Systems

Source: Adapted from Chapanis (1982).

structuring and organizing the subtopics of this chapter, which are described briefly below and treated in detail in subsequent sections.

1. The Users. Beginning with the users is a natural starting point for any discussion of the human factors involved in computer systems. Focusing on users implies what is sometimes referred to as user-oriented design, rather than machine-oriented design. Perhaps the most important questions about users are "Who exactly are the users?" "What are their characteristics?" and "How can user requirements be translated into design requirements?"

2. The Task. The second element is the task or the job that the user has to do with the computer. The complexity of the job, the kinds of information the operator needs to perform the job, and the constraints under which jobs must be performed are all relevant considerations in the human factors design of computer systems. Task requirements are discussed in the section on users.

3. The Hardware. Hardware means input devices, output display, and signaling devices, and the work station that the computer operator has to use.

4. The Software. Software generally refers to the data bases, computer programs, and procedures available in a computer system.

5. Procedures. Procedures, manuals, and documentation are often included under software. They are shown separately in Figure 5-1 because the problems associated with manuals and documentation are somewhat different from those associated with programming languages, commands, and menus.

6. The Work Environment. Generally speaking, computers and computer systems are found in relatively benign work environments. Nonetheless, some features of the work environment--excessive glare, noise, and sometimes dirt and vibration--have to be considered in the design of the user-computer interface. Since standard human factors recommendations and good engineering practice are usually adequate guides for designing most work environments in which computers are located, we do not cover environmental variables in this chapter.

USERS AND TASKS

Computer users today are almost as varied as people in general. Although there have been a number of attempts

to categorize or classify computer users into various
groups or along various dimensions, there is today no
generally accepted way of doing either. Computer tasks,
by contrast, can be classified under the same headings as
are used in task analyses. Proceeding from the more
global to the more detailed they are jobs, functions,
tasks, and subtasks. According to Ramsey and Atwood
(1979), most of the literature about computer tasks is at
the job level. Some people think, however, that computer
tasks cannot be classified in isolation, but that tasks
interact with users and that the two must be treated
together. Examples are: professional programmers designing systems, professionals using application programs
with command languages, occasional users using application
programs with menus. In short, classifying computer users
and tasks is clearly in need of systematic work, and it is
treated more fully in the sections that follow. We rely
in our discussion on the exemplary review of the literature on human-computer interaction by Ramsey and Atwood
(1979), which was supported by the Office of Naval
Research.

Users

Attempts to classify users have followed one of several
quite different approaches. The first is to categorize
users into more-or-less distinct groups on the basis of
their familiarity or sophistication with computers. This
way of classifying users has yielded a large collection
of names. Examples, in alphabetical order, are: casual
users (Martin, 1973), computer professionals (Barnard et
al., 1981), dedicated users (Martin, 1973), discretionary
users (Bennett, 1979), experienced users (Shackel, 1981),
familiar users (Ledgard et al., 1981), first-time users
(Al-Awar et al., 1981), the general public (Shackel,
1981), general users (Miller and Thomas, 1977), inexperi-
enced users (Dzida et al., 1978), naive users (Thompson,
1969), noncomputer specialists (Shackel, 1981), nonpro-
grammers (Martin, 1973), occasional users (Hammond et
al., 1980), programmers (Martin, 1973), regular users
(Dzida et al., 1978), and untrained users (Martin, 1973).

Another way of categorizing users has focused more on
the nature of the user's job. This has produced such
categories as: analysts (S. L. Smith, 1981), clerical
workers (Stewart, 1974), managers (Eason, 1974), operators
(Smith, 1981), programmers (Martin, 1973), rugged opera-

tors (Martin, 1973), service personnel (Smith, 1981), specialists (Stewart, 1974), and technical users (Ramsey and Atwood, 1979).

Quite a different way of classifying users is in terms of underlying personal characteristics. Thus, Ramsey and Atwood suggest obtaining data about users' abilities, acquired skills, general background (including formal education), sex, age, attitude measures, mechanical (perhaps also spatial) aptitudes, vocabulary test performance, recency and length of training periods, training scores, cognitive decision style, and general intelligence.

Another classification of users' characteristics would include data on the following:

1. Sensory capacities, e.g., visual acuity
2. Motor abilities, e.g., typing skills
3. Anthropometric dimensions, for hardware design
4. Intellectual capacities, e.g., general intelligence and special abilities in order to evaluate reading levels for information presented
5. Learned cognitive skills, including familiarity with the English language
6. Mathematical and logical skills
7. Experience with computers and proficiency in training
8. Personality, e.g., attitudes toward computers

Shneiderman (1980), by contrast, classifies users only according to their semantic and syntactic knowledge about computers. This way of classifying users yields the simple matrix shown in Figure 5-2.

The diversity of approaches that have been taken to this problem indicates that we need research to understand and identify which of many possible user characteristics are important for software design. In addition, research is needed to understand how to express and translate user characteristics into terms that can be used in systems design, i.e., into specifications for designers of system software.

It is important to recognize that all users, whether they are seasoned systems programmers or less experienced users, continue to learn as newer systems are developed and/or updated. For that reason, Cuff (1980) has suggested that we need to consider the casual user of computers as well as expert or naive users. Additional dimensions of user behaviors could give us evidence of the functionality of systems, e.g., the range of tasks

SYNTACTIC KNOWLEDGE

	little	a lot
little	Naive user	Data entry job control language (JCL) novices
a lot	Infrequent novice user	Frequent professional user

SEMANTIC KNOWLEDGE (row labels)

FIGURE 5-2 Classification of Users According to the Extent of Their Semantic and Syntactic Knowledge

Source: Adapted from Shneiderman (1980).

users can perform with a given system, how long it takes a user to learn a system or a system update, and the time it takes a user to perform a particular task or job. We need to know what kinds of errors users make when learning new systems as well as how many errors are made and how often they are made or repeated, how well users adapt to changes in system software (robustness) that are "upward compatible,"* and how users rate subjectively the quality of the output or product and the systems that perform their set of tasks.

When we look at what is currently known about the novice compared with the expert user, it appears that the former is generally engaged in problem solving and is very susceptible to task-structure variations. The expert systems programmer typically interacts with a computer as a routine cognitive skill and is somewhat immune to structural variations in the tasks performed (see Moran,

---

*Upward compatible means that commands and features used in an older version of software are still available in a newer version, although the newer version may provide new commands or features that are more efficient for accomplishing the same ends.

1981; Mayer, 1981). A simple dialog in the software that is computer-initiated and tutorial in nature is probably more appropriate for the occasional and naive user, but an abbreviated, user-initiated dialog appears to be more appropriate for the experienced user. It is clear that we need to gather more data about problem-solving strategies and preferences across different types of tasks for different levels of users.

Of particular concern is that the research methods used in evaluating user characteristics for hardware design have been used in studies evaluating user characteristics for software design. It is not known if these research methods are appropriate for evaluating software use or which methods will provide the most information to designers. Moran (1981) has addressed this issue in part.

Perhaps the two most pressing research needs in this area are to find some meaningful way of classifying or categorizing users and translating user characteristics into specific recommendations that can be used in the design of computer hardware, software, and documentation.

Tasks

Most computer and human factors specialists agree that a task taxonomy is needed and that system designers need a set of benchmark tasks to evaluate hardware/software development and changes. A task structure provides the rules of the game that determine the range of actions users can and cannot take (Moran 1981). Tasks can vary in several ways. They may (1) fulfill different functions for the user, e.g., professional, educational, or home hobby functions, (2) require different forms of language such as natural language, BASIC, COBOL, or APL, and (3) be performed on different kinds of systems.

In addition, almost all system designers recognize that the user's interface with a computer system changes as tasks or jobs change. The user interface includes any part of the computer system that the user comes in contact with physically, perceptually, or conceptually. The user's conceptual model of the system to be used to perform a given task is part of that interface. Thus, we also need research to understand how to discover a user's conceptual model(s) when he or she is interfacing with the computer.

Models suggested by Moran (1981) involve explicit information processes that spell out step-by-step the mental operations the user must go through to complete the task application. These models need to be based on a psychological theory of users. One example of specific models that describe individual user differences in understanding calculator languages is described by Mayer and Bayman (1981).

It would be helpful if a subset of the task taxonomy or benchmark tasks could be integrated into the accounting systems of computers so that system designers could be provided with statistical data about tasks and users. These statistics on users should include information about the user type and systems used as well as errors in usage. One example of a keystroke-level model for evaluating performance is described by Card et al. (1980).

Of primary need are systematic studies of the conceptual models of users when they interact with a variety of hardware and software systems to do specified sets of tasks, e.g., text editing, numerical problem solving, or querying data bases. These studies should choose successful methodologies for producing results that can be directly applied to system design, or they should include new methods for evaluating the interactions of user characteristics with task requirements. Another pressing problem is the development of a meaningful task taxonomy that includes both behavioral and cognitive elements for a set of four or five different representative tasks.

COMPUTER HARDWARE

Computer hardware cannot be designed in isolation because the kind of hardware available on a computer terminal determines in part the kinds of dialog and the kinds of command languages that can be implemented in the system. Ideally, decisions about important aspects of computer dialogs should precede decisions about terminal hardware. In practice, the reverse often occurs. While recognizing that these interactions exist and that they are important in design, we discuss the human factors aspects of computer hardware with only passing reference to their software implications.

Input Devices

Designers of interactive computer systems can select from an array of devices for inserting information into computers. Table 5-1, modified from the work of Ramsey

TABLE 5-1 Computer Input Devices With Some of Their Principal Features and References

Input Device	Features	References
Keyboard	The vast majority of past research on input devices has dealt with keyboards. Reasonable and fairly detailed guidelines exist with respect to the physical properties of keys and keyboards and--to a lesser extent--their layout, logical properties, operating procedures, etc. Guidelines for alphabetic keyboards are particularly good, and those for numeric keypads are reasonable. Function keyboards are rather system-dependent; guidelines can specify their physical properties but can only suggest methods and basic principles for function selection and layout. It is not clear that chorded keyboards are viable except in highly specialized situations.	Alden et al. (1972) Seibel (1972)
Light pen, light gun-- a wand with a light detecting tip used to determine the specific point on a display it touches.	Light pens can be used effectively for cursor placement and text selection, command construction, and for interactive graphical dialogs in general, including drawing. There is evidence, however, that greater accuracy may be possible with a mouse in discrete tasks and with a trackball in drawing tasks. Mode mixing, as by alternating use of light pen and keyboard, can significantly disrupt performance, since the light pen must be picked up and replaced with each interval of use. Continuous use of a light pen, at least on commercially available Cathode ray tube (CRT) terminals with vertical display surfaces, can be quite fatiguing. There has been no known research on desirable physical and logical properties for light pens.	English et al. (1967)* Goodwin (1975)** Irving et al. (1976)*

Joystick--a vertical stick generally used to move a display cursor in a direction corresponding to the direction of stick movement.	There are many studies of the use of joysticks for continuous tracking tasks, but few studies of their use for discrete or continuous operand selection or graphical input tasks. The studies that have been performed have found the mouse, light pen, and trackball preferable in terms of speed, accuracy, or both. Joysticks are sometimes used for windowing and zooming control in graphical displays. No research on this topic was found, although the results of tracking studies may be applicable here. Otherwise, no clear recommendations for joystick properties have emerged, even with respect to basic issues like position versus rate versus acceleration control. These issues may be fairly task-specific.	Card et al. (1978)* English et al. (1967)* Irving et al. (1976)*
Trackball--a partially exposed ball in a fixed base rotated by the hand generally used to move a displayed cursor in a direction corresponding to the direction of movement of ball rotation.	The trackball appears to be effective for both discrete and continuous operand selection and graphical input tasks, and it may yield the best performance when graphical inputs must be alternated with keyboard input. No empirical data on physical properties were found, but some such data are thought to exist in the tracking literature.	Irving et al. (1976)*

89

TABLE 5-1 (continued)

Input Device	Features	References
Mouse--a small device rolled by hand on a surface generally used to move a displayed cursor in a direction corresponding to the direction of movement of the mouse.	Although the mouse is not in widespread use, there is evidence that it is an effective device for text selection. No data are known concerning its physical properties, or its use in other tasks.	Card et al. (1978)* Engelbart (1973) English et al. (1967)*
Graphical input tablet-- a flat surface which detects the position and movement of a hand-held stylus generally used to generate a drawing on a display.	Graphical input tablets are capable of fairly high pointing accuracy (within 0.08 cm, according to one study). They are commonly used for freehand drawing but may be inferior for discrete position input tasks. They may also involve a performance decrement due to low stimulus-response compatibility when the drawing surface is separate from the display surface.	English et al. (1967)* Myer (1968)*

Touch panel—a device which overlays the display and senses the location touched by a finger or stylus.	No empirical performance data were found dealing with the touch panel. While its inherent resolution limits may preclude serious use for fine discrete position and continuous position input, it feels natural and may become a common device for more coarse positioning and selection from lists.	Hlady (1969) Johnson (1977)
Knee control	A knee control has been used in one research study for discrete position input. It is not known to be in use otherwise and seems unlikely to see serious use.	English et al. (1967)*
Thumbwheels, switches, potentiometers	These have been studied primarily outside the computer systems domain and are discussed in standard human factors reference sources. They are not often used as input devices for interactive computer systems.	Chapanis (1972)*
Tactile input devices	Although some tactile input devices have been proposed, little human factors research has been done on them other than that concerned with prosthetics.	Noll (1972)
Psychophysiological input devices	Electromyographic signals have provided superior performance in some control tasks to joysticks and other manual control devices. Use of heart rate, keyboard response latency, electroencephalographic input, etc. is technologically feasible, although sophisticated input is not yet achievable via these methods. There are ethical and legal problems as well as technological difficulties. Significant human factors	Slack (1971) Wargo et al. (1967)*

TABLE 5-1 (continued)

Input Device	Features	References
	data were not found with respect to computer-related use of these techniques.	
Automated speech recognition	The current state of this technology limits its use to relatively simple input tasks. Even in these there are problems with different speakers, noise, etc. Although speech input seems like a very desirable and natural input mode and is clearly preferred over other communication modes for interpersonal communication, it is not clear whether it will prove to be widely applicable for human-computer interaction tasks. Very little information was found that would assist the designer in recognizing tasks for which speech input is appropriate or in selecting an appropriate speech input device.	Addis (1972)** Bezdel (1970)* Braunstein and Anderson (1961)* Chapanis (1975, 1981)** Turn (1974)
Hand printing for optical character recognition (or for subsequent entry by typist)	The constrained hand printing required for optical character recognition (OCR) input results in low input rates and sometimes high recognition-error rates as well. Although manual transcription of such data clearly cannot be avoided in many cases, the preponderance of evidence suggests that direct keyboard entry yields better performance than printing, with a little practice, even when users are not skilled typists. Some error and input rate data on hand printing exists, along with some information about the effect of various printing contraints on input performance.	Apsey (1976)* Devoe (1967)* Masterson and Hirsch (1962)* L. B. Smith (1967)* Strub (1971)*

Mark sensing	As with hand printing, this form of transcription results in lower input rates than does practiced but unskilled typing. Some error and input rate data exist. May be slightly faster than constrained hand printing.	Devoe (1967)* Kulp and Kulp (1972)*
Punched cards	Keypunching performance differs significantly from ordinary typing because of differences in both the machine and the typical data to be keyed. Some reasonably good data exist on keypunch timing and error rates.	Neal (1977)*
Touch-tone telephone	Several studies suggest that the touch-tone telephone is a satisfactory device for occasional use as a computer terminal, even by naive computer users. It seems clear, though, that it is not a satisfactory device for prolonged interaction or for significant amounts of nonnumeric input.	Miller (1974)* Smith and Goodwin (1970) Witten and Madams (1977)

*The reference contains user performance data or relatively detailed results of controlled experimental work.

**The reference presents survey or questionnaire data or summarizes experimental results.

Source: Adapted from Ramsey and Atwood (1979).

and Atwood (1979), lists 16 different kinds of input devices, comments on some of their features, and identifies the principal references to studies of these devices. Since the situation has not changed materially since the Ramsey-Atwood report was issued, its findings are still valid.

By far most of the work on computer input devices has been done on keyboards; the literature is large and varied. Seibel's chapter in the Van Cott and Kinkade (1972) handbook is a good starting point for anyone interested in these problems. Ramsey and Atwood reference a number of studies done after Seibel's chapter was written, and there is a fair amount of even newer work, e.g., Hirsch (1981) and Hornsby (1981). The available literature on keyboards is sufficient to answer most practical questions. This is no longer an area urgently in need of extensive research.

The situation with regard to alternative input devices, such as light pens, touch panels, and hand printing, is different. Most of the work that has been done on these devices has compared two or more input devices in specific applications. There are not many studies of this kind in the literature, although Card et al. (1978) did evaluate the speed and accuracy of four devices for text selection. Research is needed that will lead to a set of recommendations about the kinds of input devices that are best suited to general classes of tasks (e.g., text input, input of numerical data, selection of commands and operands from displays, discrete positional [graphical] input, and continuous positional [graphical] input) and perhaps to general classes of work environments.

A much more serious concern is that there have been practically no studies of the optimal design of input devices, except for keyboards. That is, given that a light pen is better than a keyboard for some applications, how exactly would one design the best light pen for the job? Research is clearly needed on the optimal design parameters of all input devices other than keyboards.

Voice input to computers deserves special treatment because (1) it does not involve a physical mechanism that the user manipulates as such and (2) speech as a human output is distinctly different from the movements of fingers, hands, or feet that are required for the activation of most conventional computer input devices.

Speech has a number of characteristics that theoretically make it an attractive candidate for computer inputs.

TABLE 5-2 Recommendations for the Use of Auditory and Visual Forms of Presentation

Use auditory presentation if:	Use visual presentation if:
1. The message is simple.	1. The message is complex.
2. The message is short.	2. The message is long.
3. The message will not be referred to later.	3. The message will be referred to later.
4. The message deals with events in time.	4. The message deals with location in space.
5. The message calls for immediate action.	5. The message does not call for immediate action.
6. The person's visual system is overburdened.	6. The person's auditory system is overburdened.
7. The receiving location is too bright or dark-adaptation integrity is necessary.	7. The receiving location is too noisy.
8. The job requires continual movement.	8. The job allows for a stationary position.

Source: Deatherage (1972).

to be of any practical use to a computer designer. For example, how is a designer to decide whether a message is simple or complex?

What we clearly need is a detailed, comprehensive, and quantitative set of guidelines about the precise conditions under which speech input to computers is and is not desirable. These guidelines should consider the user, the task, and the work environment in which computers are located.

Although some very good speech recognition machines are available, they have some important limitations.

It is fast, effective, versatile, flexible, and requires little effort. Moreover, almost everyone knows how to talk, so that training is generally unnecessary. One of the principal reasons why speech input is not widely used, however, is that technology has not been able to provide us with speech recognition capabilities that even begin to approximate those of human listeners. Nonetheless, the state of the art is advancing rapidly. There are now some very good speech recognition devices available and their capabilities are certain to increase greatly in the foreseeable future.

Although speech has some distinct advantages as a medium of communication, it is also easy to identify applications in which speech input to computers would not be desirable. Some of these applications involve certain kinds of users (for example, persons with speech impediments), others the task (for example, intricate mathematical and chemical formulae are not easily described orally), and still others the work environment (speech input is not very efficient in noisy environments). For more reliable guidance about applications in which the voice should or should not be used, the only source of help are recommendations comparing visual and auditory forms of presentation (see Table 5-2).

Table 5-2, and others like it in the human factors literature, suffer from four major defects. First, the recommendations are oriented more toward output devices rather than input devices--that is, they do not compare speech with other possible forms of data input. However attractive speech may appear as an input medium, some data are available suggesting that it is not necessarily the solution for all situations (see, for example, Braunstein and Anderson, 1961). Second, recommendations such as those in Table 5-2 are not specifically oriented toward computer applications. Third, these comparisons are not sufficiently comprehensive to be of much use to computer designers. For example, none of these comparisons considers in detail user characteristics or the work environment in which computers are used. Some environments have rows and rows of computer terminals in close proximity. Imagine the babble that might result if 50 operators were inputting information by voice simultaneously into computers! Finally, existing comparisons of vision and audition provide information that is too vague

First, they all are word recognition devices, that is, they do not recognize continuous speech. Second, they are capable of responding only to vocabularies of restricted size. Third, they are user-dependent, that is, they must be programmed to learn to recognize words spoken by a particular person and will generally respond accurately only to that person's voice. Speech recognition machines that can respond to connected speech or that are speaker-independent are well beyond the current state of technology.

Despite these important limitations, speech input to computers can be successful and useful. There is not, however, a good base of research findings on the conditions under which speech recognition machines can be used effectively even with their limitations. For example, how much useful work can be done with vocabularies of various sizes? How effectively can people be trained to leave pauses between words in connected speech so that individual words can be recognized? How effortful is it to speak while deliberately leaving pauses between words? If vocabularies of restricted size must be used, how effectively can one construct complex inputs with the available words? What rules of grammar and syntax must be observed if one is restricted to a limited vocabulary? What should that vocabulary be? The conditions under which speech recognition devices can be used most effectively is virtually an unexplored area of research that should be vigorously pursued. One example of research in the use of voice input to operate a distributed computer network has been conducted at the Navy Postgraduate School by Poock (1980).

Output Devices

Although teletypewriters and alphanumeric cathode ray tube (CRT) displays are the most common forms of output devices used in computer systems, there are numerous other possibilities: plasma displays; light-emitting diodes (LED) and liquid crystal displays; tactile displays; audio displays, including synthetic speech; graphical displays; laser displays; and even psychophysiological output devices. The state of the art of these various output devices is summarized in Table 5-3, which is based on Ramsey and Atwood (1979).

TABLE 5-3 Computer Output Devices With Some of Their Principal Features and References

Type of Display	Features	References
Refreshed CRT	The ordinary, refreshed Cathode ray tube (CRT) is currently the basic computer display. A good deal of data exist concerning appropriate visual properties of CRT displays. Studies that have compared user performance using CRTs with performance using other display devices, however, do not provide a satisfactory basis for selection decisions.	Shurtleff (1980)*
Storage tube CRT	For some graphical applications, direct-view storage tubes may be preferable to refreshed displays. The storage tube allows very high-density, flicker-free displays but imposes significant constraints on interactive dialog. Although information exists concerning the basic functional advantages and disadvantages of such displays, no empirical data pertaining to human factors concerns were found.	Steele (1971)
Plasma panel	Plasma panel displays are inherently "dot" or punctuate displays, and studies of symbol generation methods are relevant. Little empirical information exists on human performance aspects of plasma displays per se.	
Teletypewriter	Reasonable guidelines exist with repect to the design of teletypewriter terminals, including both physical and	Dolotta (1970)

	functional properties. See the discussion of keyboards in Table 5-1.	
Line printer	Research on typography is voluminous and directly applicable. Research dealing directly with the line printer used in computer output is scanty but consistent with findings of typographic research (e.g., mixed upper-lower case is best for reading comprehension). Guidelines are not known to exist but could be constructed with additional survey of typographic research literature. Use of line printers for "pseudographic" displays is common but little discussed in the literature. Pseudographics is an inexpensive way to convey simple graphical information and should probably be used more widely in batch applications.	Cornog and Rose (1967)* Lewis (1972)** Ling (1973) Poulton and Brown (1968)**
Laser displays	Reasonable human factors guidelines with respect to visual properties have been proposed, but these displays are not widely used.	Gould and Makous (1968)
Tactile displays	Although some tactile displays have been proposed or even developed, little human factors research has been done other than that concerned with prosthetics.	Noll (1972)
Psychophysiological displays	Psychophysiological input is technically feasible now, but psychophysiological displays are still only a topic for research.	
Large-screen displays	There is conflicting evidence with respect to the performance effects of large-group versus individual displays.	Landis et al. (1967)** Smith and Duggar

TABLE 5-3 (continued)

Type of Display	Features	References
	The main advantages of large-screen displays are a larger display area and the existence of a single display that is clearly the same for all viewers. Unfortunately, higher display content is not achievable due to the resolution limits of existing technology (e.g., light valve displays) and may be unachievable in principle, since the large-screen display usually subtends a smaller visual angle than an individual display located close to the user.	(1965)**
Speech and synthetic speech	Although speech output clearly has many advantages over other output modes for interpersonal communication, there is essentially no information on the conditions for which speech would be an appropriate computer output.	Chapanis (1975, 1981)*

*The reference presents survey or questionnaire data or summarizes experimental results.
**The rererence contains user performance data or relatively detailed results of controlled experimental work.

Source: Adapted from Ramsey and Atwood (1979).

CRT Displays

Enough research has been done on CRT displays to support guidelines for their design (Galitz, 1981; Shurtleff, 1980). Although the two handbooks available do not answer all the questions designers may have, they cover a substantial number of them. Most of their recommendations are supported by research data, and those that are not seem reasonable. The two most important unresolved questions concern the size of displays and the use of colored displays.

With regard to size, Shurtleff (1980) has devoted a chapter to questions of legibility as related to display size, but he has nothing to say about the more important question of how much information can be presented on screens of various sizes. Military applications of computer displays, for example, in cockpits, must be small by necessity. How small can they be and still be legible? How can information best be presented on small displays? The converse problem may occur when many people must view the same display. In that case the relevant questions are: How large can displays be? How can information best be presented on large displays? These are not questions relating simply to the legibility of the information presented on displays of various size; such questions can easily be resolved on the basis of available data. What is needed is research on the interactions between display size and the amount of information that can be most effectively presented.

Questions on the use of color on CRT displays is also still essentially unresolved. The advantages of color coding for identification purposes are, of course, well documented, but the long-term effects of working with colored CRT displays for data entry, inquiry, or interactive dialog are not known. Although many people seem to like colored displays, others find them annoying and garish. The scanty research evidence available seems to show that colored CRT displays produce no substantial performance benefits. More research may enable designers to make informed decisions about the possible benefits of color on CRTs versus their cost and other disadvantages.

Alternatives to CRT Displays

Very little human factors research has been done on displays other than CRTs. Of particular interest are synthetic speech displays. Computer-generated speech is now available in a variety of devices, and the quality of the speech in some of these devices is quite good. The situations in which computer-generated speech is a viable alternative to visual displays, however, are not known. Basic research paralleling that on speech input is needed to produce defensible recommendations about applications in which speech output can or should be used.

Workplace Design

Computer displays and input devices are generally assembled into work stations consisting of terminals, consoles, desks, and chairs. There is, of course, a very large and useful literature on the physical layout of workplaces (see, for example, Van Cott and Kinkade, 1972), but there is very little empirical research on work station design specifically for computer-related tasks and settings. The importance of these problems is highlighted by a great deal of literature, mostly from Europe, about complaints from workers using CRT devices (see, for example, Grandjean and Vigliani, 1980).

Similar complaints from a consortium of labor unions in the United States were received by the National Institute of Occupational Safety and Health (NIOSH) in 1979. The general nature of these complaints was that employees using CRT terminals experienced a variety of symptoms including headaches, general malaise, eyestrain, and other visual and musculoskeletal problems. In response to these complaints NIOSH conducted an extensive investigation of computer work stations in three companies in the San Francisco Bay area (Murray et al., 1981). The study consisted of four phases: (1) radiation measurements, (2) industrial hygiene sampling, (3) a survey of health complaints and psychological mood states, and (4) ergonomics and human factors measurements.

Although radiation from CRTs had long been suspected as a potential health hazard, the NIOSH study seems to have conclusively ruled it out. X-ray, ultraviolet, and radio-frequency radiation in all sites and at all work stations tested was either not detectable or was well below acceptable occupational levels. Similar negative conclusions were reached about the chemical environment. Hydrocarbon, carbon monoxide, acetic acid, and formaldehyde levels in and around work stations were not appreciably different from what one would find in an ordinary living environment.

The results of the survey of health complaints were quite different, however. They show that operators of visual display terminals (VDT) experienced a greater number of health complaints, particularly related to emotional and gastrointestinal problems, than did comparable operators who did not work with VDTs. These findings, according to the NIOSH report, demonstrate a level of emotional distress for the VDT operators that could have potential long-term health consequences. The NIOSH study concludes, however, that it is quite likely that the emotional distress shown by the VDT operators is more related to the type of work activity than to the use of VDTs per se. With the growing number of VDTs in our society, it is clearly of considerable importance to establish how much of worker complaints can be traced to VDTs and how much to other factors (Ketchel, 1981; M. J. Smith, 1981). This is a research question that urgently needs to be investigated.

The NIOSH report has more to say about the ergonomic and human factors aspects of the computer workplace than about any other aspect of computer work. Keyboard heights, table and chair designs, viewing distances and viewing angles, copy holders, and other aspects of work station design all come in for criticism. Computer work stations in America appear to be as poorly designed as those in Europe (see Grandjean and Vigliani, 1980; Brown et al., 1982), forcing operators to adopt strained postures and to contend with glare and generally substandard viewing conditions (Ketchel, 1981). Although basic data for good work station design are available, they need to be assembled in a good set of guidelines specifically oriented toward such design. This also appears to be an urgent research need.

General Problems

Three general problems relating to computer hardware have received almost no attention: (1) the design of transportable terminals and data, (2) the design of robust computer systems for military purposes, and (3) the design of computer terminals for use in unusual or exotic environments, for example, in moving vehicles or under water.

Spectacular advances in microelectronics have made it possible to package enormous computing power into small packages. The full potential of this miniaturization has not yet been realized or explored. We need human factors research leading to the design and use of transportable terminals, including input and output devices and data in the form of cassettes.

Most computer systems are designed for use in benign environments. As the use of computers becomes more common in the military services, data will be urgently needed on how to design them for the rough treatment they are almost certain to receive under operational conditions.

Vibration, high-g forces, immersion in water, and perhaps other environmental conditions affect machines as well as their operators. Certain input devices, for example, light pens or even keyboards, may be difficult or impossible to use when the computer and the operator are subjected to excessive movement, vibration, or g-forces. We have essentially no information about the usability of computers or the design of computers for use under such conditions. Although this may not be an immediate problem, it is certain to become increasingly important as computers are integrated into complex systems for use in harsh, exotic, or unusual environments.

COMPUTER SOFTWARE

Software has many different meanings to computer scientists and computer analysts who develop or use computer programs that include command languages, dialog systems, and specialized applications systems with data bases. Software may have originally been synonymous with computer programs, but in general software now consists of "the operational requirements for a system, its specifications, design, and programs, all its user manuals and guides, and its maintenance documentation" (Mills, 1980:417).

Research in human factors in software has evaluated the human-computer interface with command languages, programming languages, dialog systems, and feedback and error management. Frequently the human factors studies have emphasized ease of use and ease of learning as well as efficiency of completing the problem-solving tasks on the computer. The recent experimental and observational studies were summarized in the special issue on human factors in Computing Surveys (1981), the IBM Systems Journal (1981), and in articles in Human Factors, the International Journal of Man Machine Studies, and Ergonomics. In addition, there are exemplary technical reports, such as Williges and Williges (1981), Ledgard et al. (1981), Shneiderman (1980), and the proceedings of the Conference on Human Factors in Computer Systems (Institute for Computer Sciences and Technology, 1982). The more popular trade magazines, e.g., the April 1982 issue of BYTE, also feature articles on human factors in software design. Many authors express the need for additional careful research studies in software design and criticize many current results as incomplete and inconsistent due to poor methodology, use of subject populations limited to particular types of users (e.g., college students), inadequate experimental designs, and misuse or poor use of statistics.

Selected useful guidelines for software designers are found in Engle and Granda (1975) and the recent reports by Williges and Williges (1981) and Ehrenreich (1981). Although there exist guidelines as well as selected research studies in human factors issues in software, considerable research needs to be done in order to provide information of use to system designers of software.

The research efforts needed in human factors in software design can be divided into two areas: (1) methodological studies and (2) substantive studies of software design features for the end user. The two areas are not always independent, and some research studies require attention to both. In either case we are concerned about human factors research in software systems with which end users interact or interface, not about research in programming language design per se; this is usually the concern of the computer programmer or systems analyst.

In the methodological area, research is needed on how to develop a suitable simulation capability for the design of dialog and interface systems. We need to understand how to evaluate present software systems as well as how to mock up new systems for testing and evaluation with end users. The choice of dependent variables in evaluating software is not clear. We know little about how to collect user statistics on the ease of learning of new software, how to record errors and complex response-time metrics from end users in time-sharing systems, and how to measure user satisfaction. Research is needed on what components of usability are most important for different kinds of users and applications (see Shackel, 1981).

One of the problems in this area is that we don't know how to do research on these topics. There is no agreed-upon set of empirical methodologies for conducting research studies about software issues. The studies that have been done are frequently context-specific and/or about one or two software features and are difficult to generalize and integrate with other data in the area. Examples include evaluations of a given command asking users to translate the abbreviated form into English, effects of modifications of conditional nesting structures in FORTRAN, user efficiency of indentations to locate single bugs in PASCAL, and modifications in a language used in teaching at the University of Toronto. A research program undertaken by a multidisciplinary group at Virginia Polytechnic Institute and State University by Williges and Ehrich sponsored by the Office of Naval Research [human-computer interaction and decision behavior, NR SRO-101] is attempting to develop principles of effective human-computer interaction, including establishment of a user's model of command languages. This research is interdisciplinary and programmatic in nature. Another set of methodological studies is needed to discover how to develop guidelines and what kinds of guidelines for software characteristics are most useful for system designers and engineers; for example, Smith has described his ideas and progress in this area in the proceedings of the Conference on Human Factors in Computing Systems (Institute for Computer Sciences and Technology, 1982).

In a substantive area, research is needed to understand the control of users' input accuracy through "clever" or "novel" feedback during actual user experiences as well as what the "format structures" should be for providing feedback on errors that users make. Data needs to be collected on how best to provide effective error correction features, help messages, and what range of default procedures should be provided to aid user efficiency. We need research to evaluate how important feedback and system response time are for improving user efficiency or ease of use. There is a need for methodology and quantification of user ease and efficiency. At present, studies evaluate different types of commands in a laboratory rather than in real-use settings, and it is not clear that the most effective commands in the laboratory are applicable in applied system uses. We need information on what length of commands (one, two, or three words) or how many (enter only one and wait for system response or enter six at once) are preferred by casual users rather than expert software programmers.

A variety of studies are needed in order to evaluate how best to develop natural language dialog systems and in particular what kinds of language-based models of human communication are most appropriate for commands in operating systems, editing systems, knowledge-based systems, and query systems for human computer interactions (e.g., Reisner, 1981).

Additional reseach is needed to understand how to develop knowledge-based systems for a variety of users. Knowledge-based systems are developed by a formulation of the application problem, designing and constructing the knowledge base of expertise, developing schemes of inference, search, or problem solving, winning the confidence of experts, and evaluating the programs for production versions. Examples of knowledge-based systems, frequently referred to as expert systems, include assisting users in such tasks as: (1) deducing molecular structures from the output of mass spectrometers, (2) advising when and where to drill for ore, and (3) diagnosing blood infections. It should be noted that there are three different kinds of end users of these systems, only the first of which is a user in a conventional information retrieval system: (1) in getting answers to problems, the user as client, (2) in improving the system's knowledge, the user as a tutor, and (3) in harvesting the knowledge base, the user as pupil. A summary of recent research related to knowledge-based or expert systems can be found in L. C. Smith (1980). Some of the major features of these systems, including the schemes of inference or problem-solving approaches used in defining structures for the knowledge bases, are reviewed by Feigenbaum (1978).

A recently developed specialty is software associated with special graphics displays. At present the development of both hardware and software for graphics use are at the gadget stage. We need to know how to design software modules for graphics use, what modules are best for various graphics features in addition to points, lines, and circles, and how to mix keyboard and pen inputs in ways other than up and down arrows and drawing pad devices. Most graphic software has hierarchical levels for command use; it is unknown if different levels are needed or how many are needed and which commands are best to use at each level. Also, the best ways for interacting among the hierarchically ordered levels of commands for draw and edit and the method for terminating are unknown. We need more information about what icons, menus, and special symbols should be used in creating graphics. Methods have been developed for partitioning a display screen into multiple, sometimes overlapping windows, each monitoring an independent process. There has been very little research on how best to make use of this kind of capability. We know little about how to use color effectively for different kinds of graphics displays and applications.

Several of the above research recommendations have been recognized by Moran (1981), who also suggests that further research is needed to understand users' conceptual models in interacting with a variety of software systems. In addition, Thomas and Carroll (1981) and Miller (1981) have emphasized that the areas of most needed research are in the human-to-computer communication process, including research on the advantages and disadvantages of natural language software systems for different tasks. Computers have become more a part of all office systems today, and we need to study what impact the new computer technology has on organizations and their structures as well as the effects on decision making of the new management information systems (Federico, 1980).

As a final point, it should be noted that we need research on the interaction between hardware and software design features as new developments such as voice input and video disks become more commonly incorporated into all types of computer systems.

Important research that should be done involves first the design and analysis of new methodologies for conducting software research, and second, users' conceptual models of software systems, including natural language systems for a variety of tasks. Also, we need to understand how to develop and evaluate additional knowledge-based systems for users as client, tutor, and/or pupil. Also needed are studies conducted to understand what software features would facilitate effective use of graphics in different tasks.

DOCUMENTATION

Documentation was once defined as printed matter that describes or explains how a system of some kind works or should be used. The documentation was necessarily separate from the system unless the system itself was a thing of print on paper. In the context of the computer, however, documentation can be part and parcel of the system it describes or explains. Recent experience indicates that on-line documentation has many advantages over print-on-paper documentation. It cannot get lost or separated from the system. Inasmuch as the user is working with the computer, the computer can monitor what the user is doing and help find the parts of the documentation that are pertinent to the user's current activity and current quandary. When the user thinks he or she understands what to do the computer can help do it--and may be able to try it out in a tentative way that will not cause much trouble if the user's understanding is faulty. The possibilities are obviously revolutionary. Because on-line documentation is relatively new, however, not much is known about how to design and implement it effectively. Clearly the first priority for research in documentation is to explore, evaluate, and improve techniques of on-line documentation.

On-line documentation within the system is not the answer to all needs for documentation, of course. Some computer systems (such as batch-processing systems and automatic process-control systems) are noninteractive, and others (such as many avionics systems) do not have enough memory or storage to make on-line documentation feasible. Documentation for such systems is, by and large, not very satisfactory. There is still need, therefore, for improved external documentation, documentation that is associated with the system but not in it. Wright (1981) has several useful suggestions for documentation designers, including suggested aids that take the form of heuristics for analyzing the user's interaction with the text. Her suggestions also consider types of users and the user's (reader's) purpose rather than the producer designer's (writer's) purpose as a classification for documents.

Of course, external documentation need not necessarily be print-on-paper documentation. It is an interesting idea to associate a "documentation computer" with the system to which the documentation pertains. In some instances, the documentation computer might be a small machine, even a portable one, taking the place of a few manuals; other instances--those that have veritable libraries of documentation--might require a documentation computer system of significant size. In an experimental system on an aircraft carrier, for example, the computer system that handles documentation is a network of about

30 PERQs* that are 16-bit, chip-based "personal" computers of substantial capability.

Documentation as Part of an Overall System

The aircraft carrier project introduces a concept that will no doubt be very important in the future: Documentation and what users do with it are parts of a larger system. If the use of documentation leads to the discovery of a defective part, inventory must be checked and ordering may have to be done. If the use of documentation leads to isolation of a software bug, software maintenance work must be done. It would be convenient and would foster efficiency if the same system that handled documentation also handled inventory and software maintenance. To improve the overall effectiveness of documentation, research is needed on the interactions of documentation with other parts of the overall task support system.

Computer-Based Versus Print-on-Paper Documentation

The discussion thus far has focused on computer-based documentation, even when the system being documented is not itself an interactive computer system. That choice reflects the judgment that research in computer-based documentation is more likely to make a major payoff than ongoing research in print-on-paper documentation. The latter research has led to many improvements and the total effect has been significant, but, insofar as conventional documentation is concerned, diminishing returns have set in. Computer-based documentation, by contrast, with the capability of the computer, offers hope of a very major advance. While computer-based documentation is not a new concept by any means, it has just recently begun to be studied systematically. The "help systems" and the "tutorials" of the 1960s and 1970s were written without the benefit of research of the kind that was devoted, for example, to programming languages. As a result, it has been said, the help systems needed help systems and the tutorials needed tutors. Our

---

*PERQ is a trademark of the Three Rivers Computer Corporation.

conclusion is that now is the time to make a strong research attack on computer-based documentation, including self-instructional programs, coherent system-wide help systems, documentation keyed to the behavior of programs (so that an error calls forth an explanation of what went wrong), and programming languages that write programs to explain themselves.

Capturing the Intent of the Creators of the System

As suggested earlier, documentation must be viewed as a part of the overall system that interacts with other parts of the overall system. The time dimension--the history--of the overall system is a very important base of the interaction. Most systems are developed through efforts to improve earlier systems, and those that do not are developed from some kind of design activity in the minds of system designers. (Programs are systems, of course, so the same can be said of programs). The intentions of the improvers and designers are crucially important to understanding what the systems do, how they work, and how they should be used--but intentions tend not to be captured in the plans and designs. A computer program, for example, usually tells how to do something, not what it is that is being done, and it is very difficult to reconstruct the programmer's intentions from the program. Research on this topic may or may not improve the situation, but it clear that the situation needs to be improved. A broad view of documentation is important. The right approach may be to create computer-based design and upgrading metasystems, within which improvers and designers would work under constant monitoring, with as much emphasis on recording intentions and goals as on devising the means for achieving them. Note that this notion, if not developed with sensitivity to privacy issues, could lead to serious ethical problems.

Dynamic Graphics and Documentation

Although documentation was, in earlier days, primarily print on paper, some documentation has been available in other media, such as recorded speech and movies. The latter offered, at considerable cost, the advantages of kinematic graphics and moving gray-scale and color pictures. The computer promises to reduce the cost of preparing kinematic graphics by having a single, static program create dynamic multidimensional patterns that develop over time. The video disk promises to reduce the cost of storing and playing back all kinds of information, especially pictorial information. Together the computer and the video disk may open up a new era for dynamic graphic documentation. At present the computer can select and present in a few milliseconds any one of the approximately 55,000 pictures on a video disk. It can run off sequences of continuous frames as a movie or skip around under program control and show fast slide sequences. What it selects can be conditioned, of course, by the responses of the viewer or viewers. These capabilities present an exciting opportunity to explore and develop new approaches to documentation.

Another exciting opportunity is being studied under the rubric of program visualization. The computer is capable, of course, of displaying representations of its own internal operation. It can present sequences of symbols representing the program that is being executed and the data on which the program is operating. Alternatively, it can present graphs, diagrams, and pictures to tell the person at the console what the program should be doing and what it is in fact doing. This latter approach to documentation, which requires sophisticated graphic display not widely available in the past, is now economically as well as technically feasible. The hope is that iconic displays will prove superior to symbolic displays in presenting the broad picture of the behavior of computer programs and systems and in helping people deal with their intrinsic complexity. With the iconic approach, it may be possible to provide something analogous to a zoom lens, through which one would be able to monitor and control the broad picture as long as everything proceeds according to plan, then focus on the offending details as soon as trouble arises.

Documentation in the Form of Knowledge Bases

Conventional documentation takes the forms of natural language text, diagrams, sketches, pictures, and tables of data; it is designed exclusively to be read by eye. New forms of documentation are becoming essential: pointer structures, semantic networks, procedural networks, and production rules, documentation designed to be

interpreted by computer programs. Such documentation
will probably be used first in interactive computer
systems to help end users or programmers and maintenance
workers, but in due course it will be used also in fully
automatic systems sophisticated enough to read their own
documentation and restructure themselves to overcome
difficulties and maximize performance. Some work has
already been done on such documentation in the field of
artificial intelligence; much more needs to be done. It
is essential to couple research on documentation closely
with other research pertinent to the systems in which it
will be used--for example, with work on interactive
tutorial systems for end users, interactive maintenance
systems, and robotic maufacturing systems.

Computer Systems to Facilitate Conventional Documentation

The foregoing emphasis on computer-based documentation
expresses our conviction that it is the high-payoff area
within the documentation field, but it should not be
taken to imply that conventional documentation is dead.
We think that two main foci have the greatest potential
payoff for research in conventional documentation: (1)
understanding the target group of people that the documentation is intended to help and the tasks in which
they will be engaged when they use the documentation and
(2) using computer systems, with good editors, formatters,
and composers to facilitate creation and production of
conventional documentation.

The theme of understanding the users is developed
elsewhere in this chapter. Great advances have been made
in the last few years in the design of computer-based
systems for creating and producing conventional documents,
and research in that area has much new technology to work
on. Indeed, research is needed to develop the capability
to make the new editors, formatters, and composers easy
to use in order to facilitate the preparation of documentation that will make them and other systems easy to
use. Kruesi, for example, supported by the Office of
Naval Research (NR 196-160), is investigating the
relationship between the types of documentation provided
to programmers and their performance on a wide variety of
software-related tasks.

In summary, research should be emphasized in several
areas pertinent to documentation: (1) techniques of

on-line documentation, (2) interactions and information flows between document subsystems and other subsystems, (3) efforts to capture the intent of designers and upgraders of systems, (4) dynamic graphics and the video disk, (5) dynamic graphics and program visualization, (6) knowledge bases, (7) understanding the uses and users of documentation, and (8) computer-based systems for the development of conventional documentation. Of these suggestions two primary research needs are to know how and when to use display documentation with graphics and what program visualization techniques are most helpful to users.

SUMMARY AND CONCLUSIONS

The primary research recommendatons in the areas of users, tasks, hardware, software, and documentation include a major emphasis on developing new methodologies to evaluate what is meant by ease of use in human-computer interaction. Does ease of use mean the extent to which it is easy to learn to use a computer; does it imply good design of hardware and software for a variety of naive, casual, and professional users; does it mean that any task can be done quickly and without errors; does it encompass a component of judged satisfaction about use; or does it mean all of these?

We need to know what user characteristics are important determinants of successful human-computer interaction for a specified set of tasks, such as data base inquiries, computation and accounting problems, and editor or word processing functions. In the area of hardware design, more research is needed to evaluate alternatives to keyboard input (including voice input), uses of color in displays, the best sizes of displays, and alternatives to CRT displays. Studies in evaluating software are barely beginning to provide data for design use. We don't yet know how to conduct systematic research studies in software design, what independent variables are most important, and what dependent variables of human-computer interaction should be recorded. We don't have data to support the design of a simulation facility to effectively evaluate commands in operating systems, editing systems, knowledge-based systems, and query systems. We need to understand users' conceptual models in interacting with specific software systems, and we need more information about the advantages and disadvantages of natural language software systems. Documentation may well become part of the available software for users; when and how to display documentation is an important area for research. Research is needed on how best to use graphics and special knowledge bases to facilitate uses of documentation either on line or in manuals. Current documentation is designer-oriented rather than user-oriented, and the perspectives should be changed so that documentation is used more effectively.

Although the research needs outlined are numerous, a major emphasis in this chapter is on systematic studies that include all four substantive variables--user and task characteristics, hardware, software, and documentation--and the interaction of these components with a clear-cut set of studies to define ease of use.

REFERENCES

Addis, T. R.
    1972   Human behaviour in an interactive environment using a simple spoken work recognizer. *International Journal of Man-Machine Studies* 4:255-284.

Al-Awar, J., Chapanis, A., and Ford, W. R.
    1981   Tutorials for the first-time computer user. *IEEE Transactions on Professional Communication* PC-24:30-37.

Alden, D. G., Daniels, R. W., and Kanarick, A. F.
    1972   Keyboard design and operation: a review of the major issues. *Human Factors* 14:275-293. (A very similar paper by the same authors is Technical Report 12180-FRIA, Honeywell Systems and Research Center, St. Paul, Minn., March 1970).

Apsey, R. S.
    1976   Human factors of constrained handprint for OCR. Pp. 466-470 in *Proceedings, IEEE International Conference on Cybernetics and Society*. November 1976. New York: Institute of Electrical and Electronics Engineers, Inc.

Barnard, P. J., Hammond, N. V., Morton, J., and Long, J. B.
    1981   Consistency and compatability in human-computer dialogue. *International Journal of Man-Machine Studies* 15:87-123.

Bennett, J. L.
  1979   Incorporating usability into system design. *Design '79 Symposium*. Monterey, Calif., April 1979.

Bezdel, W.
  1970   Some problems in man-machine communication using speech. *International Journal of Man-Machine Studies* 2:157-168.

Bigelow, R. P.
  1981   Two is the prime number in love, war, and lawsuits. *Infosystems* 28(11):92, 94.

Branscomb, Lewis M.
  1982   Electronics and computers: an overview. *Science* 215:755-760.

Braunstein, M., and Anderson, N. W.
  1961   A comparison of the speed and accuracy of reading aloud and key-punching digits. *IEEE Transactions on Human Factors in Electronics* HFE-2:56-57.

Brown, B. S., Rinalducci, E. J., and Dismukes, R. K.
  1982   *Video Display Terminals and Vision of Workers: Summary and Overview of a Symposium*. Committee on Vision, National Research Council. *Behaviour and Information Technology* 1(2):121-140.

Card, S. K., English, W. K., and Burr, B. J.
  1978   Evaluation of mouse, rate-controlled isometric joystick, step keys, and text keys for text selection on a CRT. *Ergonomics* 21:601-631.

Card, S. K., Moran, T. P., and Newell, A.
  1980   The keystroke-level model for user performance time with interactive systems. *Communications of the ACM* 23:396-410.

Chapanis, A.
  1972   Design of controls. Pp. 345-379 in H. P. Van Cott and R. G. Kinkade, eds., *Human Engineering Guide to Equipment Design*. Revised edition. Sponsored by the Joint Army-Navy-Air Force Steering Committee. Washington, D. C.: U. S. Government Printing Office.
  1975   Interactive human communication. *Scientific American* 232(3):36-42.
  1981   Interactive human communication: some lessons learned from laboratory experiments. Pp. 65-114 in B. Shackel, ed., *Man-Computer Interaction: Human Factors Aspects of*

Computers and People. Alphen aan den Rijn, The Netherlands: Sijthoff and Noordhoff.

1982 Humanizing computers. In Proceedings ITT Europe Human Factors Symposium, 18-19 May. London: ITT Europe Engineering Support Centre, 20-53.

Cornog, D. Y., and Rose, F. C.
1967 Legibility of Alphanumeric Characters and Other Symbols: II. A Reference Handbook. National Bureau of Standards Miscellaneous 262-2. Washington, D. C.: U. S. Government Printing Office.

Cuff, R.
1980 On casual users. International Journal of Man-Machine Studies 12:163-187.

Deatherage, B. H.
1972 Auditory and other sensory forms of presentation. Pp. 123-160 in H. P. Van Cott and R. G. Kinkade, eds., Human Engineering Guide to Equipment Design. Revised edition. Washington, D. C.: U. S. Government Printing Office.

Dertouzos, M. L., and Moses, J.
1980 The Computer Age: A Twenty-Year View. Cambridge, Mass.: MIT Press.

Devoe, D. B.
1967 Alternatives to handprinting in the manual entry of data. IEEE Transactions on Human Factors in Electronics HFE-8:21-32.

Dolotta, T. A.
1970 Functional specifications for typewriter-like time-sharing terminals. Computing Surveys 2:5-31.

Dzida, W., Herda, S., and Itzfeldt, W. D.
1978 User-perceived quality of interactive systems. IEEE Transactions on Software Engineering SE-4:270-276.

Eason, K. D.
1974 The manager as a computer user. Applied Ergonomics 5:9-14.

Ehrenreich, S. L.
1981 Query languages: design recommendations derived from the human factors literature. Human Factors 23:709-726.

Engelbart, D. C.
1973 Design considerations for knowledge workshop terminals. AFIPS Conference Proceedings 42:221-227.

Engle, Stephen E., and Granda, Richard E.
1975   Guidelines for Man/Display Interfaces. IBM Poughkeepsie Laboratory Technical Report TR 00.2720, December 19, 1975.

English, W. K., Engelbart, D. C., and Berman, M. L.
1967   Display-selection techniques for text manupulation. IEEE Transactions on Human Factors in Electronics HFE-8:5-15.

Federico, Pat-Anthony
1980   Management Information Systems and Organizational Behavior. New York: Praeger.

Feigenbaum, Edward A.
1978   The art of artificial intelligence--themes and case studies of knowledge engineering. In Sakti P. Ghosh and Leonard Y. Liu, eds., Proceedings of the American Federation of Information Processing Societies. Volume 47. Montvale, N. J.: AFIPS Press.

Galitz, W. O.
1981   Handbook of Screen Format Design. Wellesley, Mass.: Q.E.D. Information Science, Inc.

Gantz, J., and Peacock, J.
1981   Computer systems and services for business and industry. Fortune 103(8):39-84 (advertisement).

Goodwin, N. C.
1975   Cursor positioning on an electronic display using lightpen, lightgun, or keyboard for three basic tasks. Human Factors 17:289-295.

Grandjean, E., and Vigliani, E., eds.
1980   Ergonomic Aspects of Visual Display Terminals. London: Taylor and Francis.

Hammond, N. V., Long, J. B., Clark, I. A., Barnard, P. J., and Morton, J.
1980   Documenting human-computer mismatch in the interactive system. Proceedings of the Ninth International Symposium on Human Factors in Telecommunications. Holmdel, N. J., September 17-24, 1980.

Hirsch, R. S.
1981   Procedures of the human factors center at San Jose. IBM Systems Journal 20:123-171.

Hlady, A. M.
1969   A touch sensitive X-Y position encoder for computer input. AFIPS Conference Proceedings 35:545-551.

Hornsby, M. E.
   1981   A comparison of full- and reduced-alpha keyboards for aircraft data entry. P. 257 in *Proceedings of the Human Factors Society, 25th Annual Meeting.*

Institute for Computer Sciences and Technology, National Bureau of Standards, and Washington, D. C., Chapter, Association for Computing Machinery
   1982   Proceedings: Human Factors in Computer Systems. March 15-17, Gaithersburg, Md.

Irving, G. W., Horinek, J. J., Walsh, D. H., and Chan, P. Y.
   1976   *ODA Pilot Study II: Selection of an Interactive Graphics Control Device for Continuous Subjective Functions Applications.* Report No. 215-2. Santa Monica, Calif.: Integrated Sciences Corp.

Johnson, J. K.
   1977   Touching data. *Datamation* 23(1):70-72.

Ketchel, J.
   1981   Visual display terminal research--the opportunity and the challenge. *Human Factors Society Bulletin* 24(10):2-3.

Kulp, R. A., and Kulp, M. J.
   1972   A comparison of mark sensing and handprinting coding methods. Pp. 416-421 in *Proceedings of the Sixteenth Annual Meeting of the Human Factors Society.* Santa Monica, Calif.: Human Factors Society.

Landis, D., Slivka, R. M., Jones, J. M., Harrison, S., and Silver C. A.
   1967   *Evaluation of Large Scale Visual Displays.* Technical Report No. RADC-TR-67-57. Griffiss AFB, Rome, N. Y.: Rome Air Developmental Center. (NTIS No. AD 651372)

Ledgard, H., Singer, A., and Whiteside, J.
   1981   Directions in human factors for interactive systems. In *Lecture Notes in Computer Science* 103. New York: Springer-Verlag.

Lewis, R. A.
   1972   Legibility of capital and lowercase computer printout. *Journal of Applied Psychology* 56:280-281.

Ling, R. F.
   1973   A computer generated aid for cluster analysis. *Communications of the ACM* 16:355-361.

Martin, J.
　1973　*Design of Man-Computer Dialogues*. Englewood Cliffs, N. J.: Prentice-Hall.

Masterson, J. L., and Hirsch, R. S.
　1962　Machine recognition of constrained handwritten Arabic numbers. *IEEE Transactions on Human Factors in Electronics* HFE-3:62-65.

Mayer, Richard E.
　1981　The psychology of how novices learn computer programming. *Computing Surveys* 13:121-141.

Mayer, R. E., and Bayman, P.
　1981　Psychology of calculator languages: a framework for describing differences in users' knowledge. *Communications of the ACM* 24:511-520.

Miller, L. A.
　1974　Programming by non-programmers. *International Journal of Man-Machine Studies* 6:237-260.
　1981　Natural language programming: styles, strategies, and contrasts. *IBM Systems Journal* 20:184-215.

Miller, L. A., and Thomas, J. C.
　1977　Behavioral issues in the use of interactive systems. *International Journal of Man-Machine Studies* 9:509-536.

Mills, H. D.
　1980　Management of software engineering systems, Part I. Principles of Software Engineering. *IBM Systems Journal* 19:415-420.

Moran, Thomas P.
　1981　An applied psychology of the user. *Computing Surveys* 13:1-11.

Murray, W. E., Moss, C. E., and Parr, W. H.
　1981　A radiation and industrial hygiene survey of video display terminal operations. *Human Factors* 23:413-420.

Murray, W. E., Moss, C. E., Parr, W. H., Cox, C., Smith, M. J., Cohen, B. F. G., Stammerjohn, L. W., and Happ, A.
　1981　*Potential Health Hazards of Video Display Terminals*. U. S. Department of Health and Human Services, Public Health Service, Center for Disease Control, National Institute of Occupational Safety and Health, Division of Biomedical and Behavioral Science, Division of Surveillance, Hazard Evaluations and Field Studies. Washington, D. C.: U. S. Government Printing Office.

Myer, T. H.
   1968   How well do people point? <u>Grafacon Interface</u> 2 (Bolt Beranek & Newman Inc., Cambridge, Mass.).

Neal, A. S.
   1977   Time intervals between keystrokes, records, and fields in data entry with skilled operators. <u>Human Factors</u> 19:163-170 (Also: Technical Report HFC-8. San Jose, Calif.: IBM Corp., System Development Division, Human Factors Center, October 1974).

Nickerson, R. S.
   1969   Man-computer interaction: a challenge for human factors research. <u>Ergonomics</u> 12:501-517.

Noll, A. M.
   1972   Man-machine tactile communication. <u>SID Journal</u> 1(2):5-11.

Poock, Gary K.
   1980   Experiments with Voice Input for Command and Control: Using Voice Input to Operate a Distributed Computer Network. Technical Report, Navy Electronic Systems Command, Washington, D. C.

Poulton, E. C., and Brown, C. H.
   1968   Rate of comprehension of an existing teleprinter output and of possible alternatives. <u>Journal of Applied Psychology</u> 52:16-21.

Ramsey, H. R., and Atwood, M. E.
   1979   <u>Human Factors in Computer Systems: A Review of the Literature</u>. Technical Report SAI-79-111-DEN, 21 September 1979. Engelwood, Colo.: Science Applications, Inc.

Reisner, Phyllis
   1981   Human factors studies of database query languages. A survey and assessment. <u>Computing Surveys</u> 13:13-32.

Rupp, B. A.
   1981   Comments on certain German video display terminal regulations. <u>Human Factors Society Bulletin</u> 24(10):3-4.

Seibel, R.
   1972   Data entry devices and procedures. Pp. 311-344 in H. P. Van Cott and R. G. Kinkade, eds., <u>Human Engineering Guide to Equipment Design</u>. Revised ed. Washington, D. C.: U.S. Government Printing Office.

Shackel, Brian
   1981   The Concept of Usability. Paper presented at the Software and Information Usability Symposium, IBM, Poughkeepsie, N.Y. (15-18 September 81) and at the ITT Symposium on Human Factors and the Usability of Software, ITT Advanced Technology Center, Shelton, Conn. (5 Oct 81).

Shneiderman, Ben
   1980   <u>Software Psychology: Human Factors in Computer and Information Systems</u>. Cambridge, Mass.: Winthrop Publishers.

Shurtleff, D. A.
   1980   <u>How To Make Displays Legible</u>. La Mirada, Calif.: Human Interface Design.

Slack, W.
   1971   Computer-based interviewing system dealing with nonverbal behavior as well as keyboard responses. <u>Science</u> 171:84-87.

Smith, L. B.
   1967   A comparison of batch processing and instant turnaround. <u>Communications of the ACM</u> 10:495-500.

Smith, L. C.
   1980   Artificial intelligence applications in information systems. In Martha E. Williams, ed. <u>Annual Review of Information Science and Technology</u>. White Plains, N. Y.: Knowledge Industry Publications Inc.

Smith, M. J.
   1981   Job stress and VDT work. <u>Human Factors Society Bulletin</u> 24(10):4-5.

Smith, S. L.
   1981   The Usability of Software: Design Guidelines for the User-System Interface. Paper presented at the ITT Symposium on Human Factors and the Usability of Software, ITT Advanced Technology Center, Shelton, Conn. (5 October 1981).

Smith, S. L., and Duggar, B. C.
   1965   Do large shared displays facilitate group effort? <u>Human Factors</u> 7:237-244. (NTIS No. AD 633262)

Smith, S. L., and Goodwin, N. C.
   1970   Computer-generated speech and man-computer interaction. <u>Human Factors</u> 12:215-223.

Steele, K. A.
   1971   CPM/PERT. In *Proceedings, 2nd Man-Computer Communications Seminar*. Otawa, Canada: National Research Council of Canada, 81-84.

Stewart, T. F. M.
   1974   Ergonomic aspects of man-computer problem solving. *Applied Ergonomics* 5:209-212.

Strub, M. H.
   1971   *Evaluation of Man-Computer Input Techniques for Military Information Systems*. Technical Research Note 226. Arlington, Va.: U. S. Army Behavior and Systems Research Laboratory, May 1971. (NTIS No. AD 730315)

Thomas J. C., and Carroll, J. M.
   1981   Human factors in communication. *IBM Systems Journal* 20:237-263.

Thompson, D. A.
   1969   Man-computer system: toward balanced co-operation in intellectual activities. In *Proceedings, International Symposium on Man-Machine Systems*. IEEE Conference Record Number 69C58-MMS. Volume 1. New York: Institute of Electrical and Electronics Engineers.

Turn, R.
   1974   *Speech as a Man-Computer Communication Channel*. Report No. P-5120. Santa Monica, Calif.: Rand Corp.

U.S. Bureau of the Census
   1979   *Statistical Abstracts of the United States* 100th ed.: Table Number 685, p. 415. Washington, D. C.: U. S. Department of Commerce.

Van Cott, H. P., and Kinkade, R. G., eds.
   1972   *Human Engineering Guide to Equipment Design*. Revised edition. Sponsored by the Joint Army-Navy-Air Force Steering Committee. Washington, D. C.: U. S. Government Printing Office.

Wargo, M. J., Kelley, C. R., Mitchell, M. D., and Prosin, J. J.
   1967   *Human Operator Response Speed, Frequency, and Flexibility: A Review Analysis and Device Demonstration*. Report No. CR-874. Washington, D. C.: National Aeronautics and Space Administration.

Williges, Robert C., and Williges, Beverly H.
: 1981 Users' Considerations in Computer Based Information Systems. Technical Report CSIE-81-2. Virginia Polytechnic Institute and State University, September 1981. (NTIS No. AD A106194)

Witten, I. H., and Madams, P. H. C.
: 1977 The telephone enquiry service: a man-machine system using synthetic speech. International Journal of Man-Machine Studies 9:449-464.

Wright, P.
: 1981 Problems to be Solved When Creating Usable Documents. Paper presented at the Software and Information Usability Symposium. 15-18 Sept. IBM, Poughkeepsie, N. Y.

Zoltan, E., and Chapanis, A.
: 1982 What do professional persons think about computers? Behaviour and Information Technology 1:55-68.

6

POPULATION GROUP DIFFERENCES

Many areas of research in human factors have concentrated on systems that fit the average person. In those studies, individual differences traditionally have been treated as little more than an error problem. Thus few data are available in many areas of human factors on the interaction of different systems with variables such as ability levels or age levels. Attempts to classify, describe, predict, and exploit individual and group differences extend to the beginnings of recorded history. Some of the earliest decipherable samples of writings include references to the physical and mental differences between men and women, serfs and noblemen, slaves and masters, and barbarians and civilized persons. It was not until the nineteenth century, however, that the study of individual and group differences assumed the systematic and rigorous qualities of scientific investigation. The attempts of Sir Francis Galton (1822-1911) to describe the nature of individual differences are the foundations of what is sometimes referred to as differential psychology.

Since Galton, investigations of individual and group differences carried out by psychologists, anthropologists, and sociologists number in the hundreds of thousands. There is a psychological journal, The Journal of Cross-Cultural Psychology, entirely devoted to studies of this kind. One of the most important applications of this work in psychology has been the development of a multimillion dollar testing industry. Psychologists have devised hundreds of tests of ability, achievement,

---

The principal authors of this chapter are Irwin L. Goldstein and Alphonse Chapanis.

skills, knowledge, and personality (Buros, 1978) that are used routinely for classifying and selecting employees for thousands of jobs and occupations.*

One of the most ambitious and thorough attempts to relate individual characteristics of workers to job requirements is the <u>Dictionary of Occupational Titles</u> (U.S. Department of Labor, 1977). This compendium gives profiles of the educational, aptitude, interest, physical, and temperament characteristics required of a worker to achieve average successful job performance in thousands of occupations. The military services have tried to do something similar on a more modest scale. In the preparation of personnel requirements data, the <u>Air Force Design Handbook</u> (Air Force Systems Command, 1969) specifies that tasks should be rated along six dimensions: ambient environment, equipment characteristics, mental demands, physical demands, hazard exposure, and task criticality. Figure 6-1 shows the three levels of mental demands that may be required of people by various duties and tasks.

Although it is seldom explicitly stated, the underlying rationale of most of these classifications is that the job or the occupation is a given, a fixed quantity. The aim of personnel selection is therefore to find persons who have the abilities, skills, and other characteristics required to perform particular jobs. From the standpoint of human factors, however, a job is not a fixed quantity but rather something that can be modified and designed to fit people with varying characteristics. Thus it becomes important to know in what ways people vary and by how much. In this area there are serious gaps in our knowledge. The most thorough translation of individual difference data into design requirements has been done in the field of anthropometry, which involves measurement of the human body. It is possible to write equipment design specifications so that the equipment will fit 90 percent, 95 percent, or any other proportion of a particular user population. The information necessary to write equally precise design specifications for other human dimensions and characteristics, however, is not available.

Attempts have been made to do that, but further research is needed on this complex problem. The Air

---

*Tests are also used for other purposes, for example, diagnosing and classifying mental illnesses, but our concern here is with job-related activities.

CODE 1 requires little or no formal training, just a basic introduction to the task; ability to follow relatively simple written or oral instructions; little judgment, since only elementary decisions are involved; little concentration; little or no recall of relevant knowledge for decisions or inference; only precise determinations, such as GO/NO-GO, UP/DOWN, MORE/LESS, YES/NO, ALL/NONE, CORRECT/INCORRECT, etc.

CODE 2 requires moderate technical knowledge and training; some ability to adjust to changing situations; occasional exercise of judgment involving use of technical knowledge; ability to understand and use technical manuals; some initiative and ingenuity required; occasional recall of relevant knowledge and experience of the practical type for decisions or inferences; decisions involving somewhat detailed procedures or measurements, as in assembling, disassembling, installing, removing, inspecting, testing, operating, adjusting, computing, monitoring, servicing, etc.

CODE 3 requires a high degree of complex and varied technical knowledge, with considerable formal and informal training; a high degree of continuous concentration, with attention to advanced and involved elements of the task; continuous exercise of a high degree of judgment, with decisions based on varied and complex factors requiring understanding of underlying principles and procedures; extensive recall of relevant and precise knowledge and experience for decisions and inferences; frequent decisions at the theoretical and abstract level; precise and detailed analysis, correlating, computing, organizing, and sequencing of processes or data, as in variable emergency procedures, troubleshooting, planning, scheduling, etc.

FIGURE 6-1 Classification of the Mental Demands Made on Personnel by Duties and Tasks

Source: Air Force Systems Command (1969).

Force's six task dimensions of ambient environment, equipment characteristics, physical demands, hazard exposure, and task criticality are a good initial effort (see Table 6-1), yet the <u>Air Force Design Handbook</u> acknowledges its limitations: "Because of the broad range of equipment characteristics, complete criteria are not presented here. The following are merely suggested guidelines" (Section DN4C3, p. 13). For example, the manual states that Code 1 equipment is ". . . complex but adequately designed for ease of use. . . ." What the definition does not specify is ease of use for whom. Something that is easy for an astronaut to use may be completely beyond the capabilities of an individual with only an elementary school education. To state the problem explicitly, we do not know exactly how to design complex equipment so that it can be used with ease by people with average IQs, people with IQs as low as 80, people with fifth-grade reading abilities, or people for whom English is a second language.

THE IMPACT OF FEDERAL ANTIDISCRIMINATION LEGISLATION

Antidiscrimination legislation has focused attention on human factors issues related both to complying with legislative requirements and maintaining the productivity of a work force with greater diversity than in the past. As a result there is increased concern over the interaction of individual differences with programs such as job redesign and training as well as over organizational attitudes toward various populations (e.g., the elderly) that may constrain their performance.

As a result of the U.S. Civil Rights Act, federal guidelines have been developed concerning personnel decisions that affect protected classes, which include: American Indian or Alaskian natives, blacks not of Hispanic origin, Hispanics, and Asian or Pacific Islanders. In addition, federal legislation has made it illegal to discriminate on the basis of sex, age, or disability. Any personnel action resulting in adverse impact against any of these groups can result in litigation. In this context, personnel decisions are not limited to selection or promotion but rather refer to any personnel practice, such as job and workplace redesign, selection for training, and the use of training as a basis for promotion.

Legal actions resulting from charges of discrimination have stimulated research on the procedures necessary to assess the validity of these types of personnel practices; however, most of the emphasis has been on the establishment of procedures to validate selection tests (American Psychological Association, 1980). Similar concerns are being expressed about methodologies for evaluating training and job redesign (Bartlett, 1978). The research emphasis has been on establishing data bases, so that it is possible to design programs that do not have adverse impact.

As a consequence of antidiscrimination legislation as well as social and economic factors, people from special population groups are moving into occupations that were previously considered nontraditional for them. An example is women who are entering managerial and blue-collar jobs and the military services. The military services are also accepting more people (male and female) who have lower ability as measured by traditional academic aptitude measures. These changes in the composition of the work force and the armed services have revealed an important problem in addition to the human factors issues of designing jobs, equipment, and training to accommodate individual differences: It has only recently been recognized that organizational attitudes toward people entering nontraditional jobs may adversely affect productivity by hindering their performance and constraining occupational aspirations.

SEX AND JOB PERFORMANCE

Sheridan's (1975) description of the American Telephone and Telegraph Company's experience in placing women in craft jobs illustrates the implications of human factors for sex and job performance. Despite rigorous recruiting and comprehensive training efforts, the women recruited into a particular job dropped from training at an average rate of 50 percent, and the women who completed training usually did not last a full year on the job. A task analysis of the job indicated that the physical tasks were extremely difficult for women to perform; furthermore, this analysis determined which tasks were causing the most difficulty. Some of the most serious problems centered on the use of a ladder that weighed approximately 80 lbs. and was 14 feet long before being extended. Women had great difficulty placing the ladder against a building

TABLE 6-1 Classification of Equipment Characteristics and Task Criticality of Various Tasks

Code	Equipment Characteristics	Task Criticality
1	Equipment is simple and presents no operating or maintenance problems in relation to the Duty or Tasks; equipment complex but adequately designed for ease of use; equipment simplifies task performance; human engineering principles effectively applied to all aspects; no features impose a burden on human capabilities; etc.	Tasks that are not critical to the operation of the system or subsystem; if they are not accomplished correctly, there will be no significant effect on the operational capabilities of the system or the success of its designed mission; improper performance may have some effect on a subsystem operation, but would not jeopardize the overall system performance or mission success.
2	Human engineering characteristics marginal; access for repair or replacement possible, but difficult; some controls or displays violate minor population stereotypes; layout of controls and displays permits, but does not facilitate performance; displays moderately difficult to read or interpret; controls somewhat difficult to reach or manipulate; etc.	Tasks that are critical for subsystem operation and may result in some system degradation if not correctly performed; tasks whose failure permits some operational capability but degrades the applicable sybsystem to the extent that only partial mission success can be achieved; tasks that affect equipment which is important to the optimum capability of the system but where alternate modes may be selected; tasks whose failure would restrict the system in its primary mission, but would not prevent the selection of other targets of opportunity; tasks where malfunctions might make it impossible to deliver stores by electronic actuation but will permit manual delivery.

3	Equipment unsuitable for proper task performance; insufficient information presented in displays; displays illegible; controls extremely difficult or impossible to reach or manipulate; equipment requires three hands to operate; access for maintenance extremely difficult or impossible; etc.	Tasks that must be performed correctly since they are critical to mission success; with task failure the system may continue to work (i.e., its basic capability, such as flying, may not be affected) but its operational effectiveness is degraded to an unacceptable level or mission fulfillment is rendered impossible.
4	[Not applicable to equipment characteristics.]	Tasks which, if not performed correctly, render the system completely inoperative and incapable of performing its mission.

Source: Air Force Systems Command (1969).

because they had to apply force below the midpoint of the ladder just as the force required to raise it was increasing. A fiberglass tube was connected to the top rungs of the ladder that enabled the worker to push the ladder against the building much more easily. As a result, workers who were 5 foot 2 inches weighing 120 pounds were able to raise a 72 lb. ladder with one hand. These and other design modifications not only allowed women to perform the job but also resulted in fewer back injuries for men.

AGE AND JOB PERFORMANCE

Important considerations with regard to age and job performance are that the average age of the population is increasing and both age discrimination legislation and rulings against forced retirement are resulting in a larger number of older people in the work force. Many of these individuals will require additional training as a result of job shifts, technological changes, or simply interest in a new career. The biases operating against these people are made obvious by Britton and Thomas's (1973) study of the views of employment interviewers. They noted that 50-year-old workers were viewed as the most difficult to place during a recession, the most difficult for an employer to train, and the least able to maintain production schedules. These views are based on preconceived beliefs that older workers cannot perform as well on the job and cannot easily acquire new skills. Data relevant to these questions are virtually nonexistent; a thorough review (Fozard and Popkin, 1978) of perceptual and cognitive data analyzed by age reinforces the view that there are few data relevant to work situations. Much of that review is based on data from laboratory experiments on topics such as paired associate learning, iconic memory, and visual discrimination, making generalizations to work situations hazardous at best.

The deficient state of this research is summarized in Sheppard's (1970) generalizations about basic research on aging and job performance: The research fails to differentiate various aspects of the work situation, including physical, psychomotor, sensory, and social characteristics; most of the emphasis is on average performance, with little, if any, attention to the substantial number of individual differences; and, there is a blind faith in trend extrapolations. If workers ages 30-40 have lower morale than workers ages 20-30, it is simply assumed that workers ages 40-50 will have even lower morale.

A good example of the implications of our lack of knowledge is evidenced by the continuing controversy concerning airline pilot age, health, and performance. An Institute of Medicine (1981) report notes that although the average risk of acute incapacitation increases with age, there are large individual differences. In addition, while there are decreases in capacity, speed or accuracy of attention, memory, and intellectual skills with increasing age, there is also evidence that well-practiced skills may not show any age-related decline. The report concludes that there is a need for research on age-related changes among pilots and a need for research on pilot performance on tasks that are representative of actual work situations.

Of more immediate relevance to this report are the relationships between group variables such as age and equipment design. For example, as they age, many people require the use of bifocals. How does the use of bifocals relate to the need to read information from displays such as those found on word processing equipment? Is it possible that the displays must be designed differently or that the information must be displayed differently depending on the age of the operator? Questions such as these constitute a largely unexplored topic for research.

INTERACTIONS AMONG VARIABLES

Another serious gap in our knowledge is how various individual and group differences interact to affect job performance. For example, there are considerable data available relating aging to maximum oxygen uptake, which determines the capacity of an individual to do prolonged heavy work (Astrand and Rodahl, 1977). These data show that there is a steady decrement in aerobic power beginning at about age 20, such that a 60-year-old attains about 70 percent of the maximum of a 25-year-old. Unfortunately, there are a few data on most population differences or individual differences as they are related to work situations. McFarland and O'Doherty (1959) concluded the following regarding the relationship of aging and work performance (pp. 454-455):

> Although most studies show an unrelieved picture
> of decline in capacities, it is well to remember
> that this constantly changing balance between
> physiological and psychological impairment, on the
> one hand, and increased experience, wisdom, and
> judgment, on the other, occasionally results in
> actual improvement of capacities, especially in
> those functions which are of greatest importance
> in daily living.

These and other interactions of variables are another almost completely untapped area of research.

NATIONAL AND ETHNIC DIFFERENCES

There are, of course, other important differences in population characteristics that should be considered in job redesign and training systems. National and ethnic differences have implications for equipment design that have just recently begun to be investigated (Chapanis, 1975). These differences are reflected in anthropometric, physiological, psychological, language, and cultural variables that affect equipment design.

For example, Ruffell-Smith (1975) notes that telegraph systems were originally used as communication devices in air traffic control systems; however, with the increased amount of speed of air traffic, voice communication systems replaced telegraph devices. Obviously, the use of the different languages of the many nations involved in air travel was a serious impediment to the operation of voice systems. After World War II English was chosen as the language of use because at that time most aircraft were operated by English-speaking countries. Yet there is a wide variation in English dialects and pronunciation, to the extent that some dialects, such as that spoken in Newcastle, are not understood by people elsewhere in the British Isles. Obviously the problems are more severe when the speaker's native language is not English. Ruffell-Smith's analysis of communication errors indicates that this problem can be serious in air traffic communication, especially when the speed of reaction is a critical element in avoiding an accident. Clearly, the implications of these population differences should be considered in design decisions.

<u>Ethnic Variables in Human Factors Engineering</u> (Chapanis, 1975) provides other examples of equipment

design complexities caused by language differences. One chapter (Hanes, 1975) shows the variety of accounting keyboards that have been designed to accommodate some of the European and Mideast languages. Another chapter (Brown, 1975) illustrates the design problems that were encountered in designing a computer terminal for Japanese, a language that is markedly different from the Indo-European languages. In general, there is little appreciation of the problems involved in designing equipment for diverse national and ethnic groups. The <u>Human Engineering Guide to Equipment Design</u> (Van Cott and Kinkade, 1972) is the best single source of human factors data available, yet it is almost entirely concerned with American and European data. It is necessary to learn to what extent its data and design recommendations need to be modified or supplemented for international use.

INDIVIDUAL DIFFERENCES AND TRAINING

Closely related to problems of equipment design are those associated with the training of individuals to operate complex equipment. Here again our information is seriously deficient. An approach that has some promise is the aptitude-treatment interaction (ATI) model. The goal of this approach is to match a particular mode of instruction to an individual's distinctive characteristics so that each person is assigned the most appropriate learning procedure. A disordinal aptitude-treatment interaction is one in which individuals with high aptitude perform best with one treatment (e.g., training or display), while those with lower aptitude perform best with another treatment. Thus, the aptitude level of the individual determines the form of treatment that has the best chance of success. Aptitude in this context refers to any personal characteristics that relate to learning and so can include a broad range of variables, such as styles of thought, personality, and various scholastic aptitudes. Treatment has typically referred to instructional modes like programmed instruction, computer-assisted instruction, visual versus verbal presentations, etc; it can be generalized, however, to any intervention, including job redesign.

An exhaustive review of this appealing strategy is provided in the text by Cronbach and Snow (1977). They examined a large number of potential aptitudes, such as learning rates, abilities, and personality, and considered their interactions with various instructional techniques. While early reviews of this topic were more pessimistic, Cronbach and Snow's extensive review and reanalyses of data have led them to conclude that aptitude treatment interaction effects are real phenomena. They note that the findings that most clearly suggest ATI effects are those dependent on prior learning experience: The technique that works best is the one that an individual has already experienced. However, ATI effects have not often been generalized or replicated. Goldstein (1980) notes the need for systematic empirical and theoretical research that matches individual differences among learners to various instructional strategies. The haphazard assignment of individuals with particular abilities to any available instructional technique is not likely to produce dividends.

BARRIERS TO SUCCESSFUL PERFORMANCE

Another important topic is the identification of barriers to successful performance for different groups. For example, some employment interviewers perceive women as more likely to be absent and to have fewer skills, even though they have no evidence to support these beliefs (Britton and Thomas, 1973). Similarly, the elderly are viewed as difficult to train (Britton and Thomas, 1973). Researchers concerned with these issues emphasize that the identification of organizational constraints, in military organizations for example, is a first step in understanding and resolving their serious retention problem. One study (Boyd et al., 1975) of 1,573 women in their first tour in the Army's basic training program was critical of the program's failure to provide realistic expectations about the training process. Subsequent to the basic training program supervisors reported the main difference between good and poor performers was job-related attitudes (discipline, following orders, military courtesy) that were not adequately presented in basic training.

RECOMMENDATIONS FOR RESEARCH
ON POPULATION GROUP DIFFERENCES

A research program to explore issues concerning population group and individual differences would need to take several approaches:

(1) It is necessary to conduct literature reviews and examinations of reports that forecast which type of population group variables (such as age and sex) and which type of work situation parameters (such as visual displays on a word processor) will be important in the future.

(2) It is necessary to collect and examine available theories and empirical data about the relevant parameters (e.g., changes in information processing capability as a function of age).

(3) Research should be sponsored on a number of topics:
- The relationship between population group variables and performance on relevant work tasks.
- The interaction between population group differences and various interventions, such as job redesign and training.
- The specification of design changes based on research findings resulting from these research recommendations.

(4) In addition, data should be collected and analyzed to identify and remove organizational constraints that serve as barriers to the successful performance of various population groups, such as women and aged and handicapped people.

REFERENCES

Air Force Systems Command
    1969   <u>AFSC Design Handbook, Series 1-10, General; AFSC DH 1-3; Personel Subsystems</u>. First edition. Andrews Air Force Base, Washington, D.C.: Air Force Systems Command.

American Psychological Association, Division of Industrial/Organizational Psychology
    1980   <u>Principles for the Validation and Use of Personnel Selection Procedures</u>. Second edition. Berkeley, Calif.: American Psychological Association.

Astrand, P. O., and Rodahl, K.
    1977   <u>Textbook of Work Physiology</u>. New York: McGraw Hill.

Bartlett, C. J.
    1978   Equal employment opportunity issues in training. <u>Human Factors</u> 20:179-188.

Boyd, H. A., Dufilho, L. P., Hungerland, J. E., and Taylor, J. E.
   1975   Performance of First-Hour WAC Enlisted Women: Data Base for the Performance Orientation of Women's Basic Training. HumRRO Technical Report, FR-WD-CA 75-10. Alexandria, Va.

Britton, J. O., and Thomas, K. R.
   1973   Age and sex as employment variables: views of employment service interviewers. *Journal of Employment Counseling* 10:180-186.

Brown, C. R.
   1975   Human factors problems in the design and evaluation of key-entry devices for the Japanese language. In A. Chapanis, ed., *Ethnic Variables in Human Factors Engineering*. Baltimore, Md.: Johns Hopkins University Press.

Buros, O. K., ed.
   1978   *The Eighth Mental Measurements Handbook*. Highland Park, N.J.: Gryphon.

Chapanis, A., ed.
   1975   *Ethnic Variables in Human Factors Engineering*. Baltimore, Md.: Johns Hopkins University Press.

Cronbach, L. J., and Snow, R. E.
   1977   *Aptitudes and Instructional Methods*. New York: Irvington.

Fozard, J. L., and Popkin, S. J.
   1978   Optimizing adult development: ends and means of an applied psychology of aging. *American Psychologist* 33:975-989.

Goldstein, I. L.
   1980   Training in work organizations. *Annual Review of Psychology* 22:565-602.

Hanes, L. F.
   1975   Human factors in international keyboard arrangement. In A. Chapanis, ed., *Ethnic Variables in Human Factors Engineering*. Baltimore, Md.: Johns Hopkins University Press.

Institute of Medicine, National Academy of Sciences
   1981   *Airline Pilot Age, Health and Performance*. Washington, D.C.: National Academy Press.

McFarland, R. A., and O'Doherty, B. M.
   1959   Work and occupational skill. In J. E. Birren, ed., *Handbook of Aging and the Individual*. Chicago: University of Chicago Press.

Ruffell-Smith, H. P.
   1975   Some problems of voice communication for international aviation. In A. Chapanis, ed., Ethnic Variables in Human Factors Engineering. Baltimore, Md.: Johns Hopkins University Press.

Sheppard, H. L.
   1970   On age discrimination. In H. L. Sheppard, ed., Towards an Industrial Gerontology. Cambridge, Mass.: Schenkman.

Sheridan, J. A.
   1975   Designing the Work Environment. Paper presented at the American Psychological Association, Chicago.

U. S. Department of Labor
   1965   Dictionary of Occupational Titles. Fourth edition. Washington, D.C.: U.S. Department of Labor.

Van Cott, H. P., and Kinkade, R. G., eds.
   1972   Human Engineering Guide to Equipment Design. Revised edition. Washingon, D.C.: U.S. Government Printing Office.

7

APPLIED METHODS IN HUMAN FACTORS

As part of an engineering team, human factors specialists apply their knowledge and skills to system definition, design, development, and evaluation in order to optimize the capabilities and performance of human-machine combinations. Their task can be formidable in complex system development. For example, military standard MIL-H-46855B of the Department of Defense details the human factors requirements that must be addressed in the development of military systems; an outline of these requirements appears as Figure 7-1. The outline is also a reasonable representation of the human factors considerations that may be relevant to the development of any system.

In designing and creating systems human factors specialists use a variety of analytic and data-gathering techniques to assess problems, develop machine and human requirements and functions, and evaluate system or subsystem performance. Although many of these problems would ideally be solved with the experimental methods

---

The principal authors of this chapter are Alphonse Chapanis and Robert T. Hennessy. It is based on a workshop on applied methods held in December 1981 under the sponsorship of the Committee on Human Factors. The workshop participants and, therefore, the principal contributors to this chapter are Alphonse Chapanis (workshop chairman), Johns Hopkins University; Stuart K. Card, Xerox Palo Alto Research Center; David Meister, US Navy Personnel Research and Development Center; Donald L. Parks, Boeing Aerospace Company; Richard W. Pew, Bolt Beranek & Newman Inc.; Erich P. Prien, Memphis State University; John B. Shafer, IBM Corporation; and Robert T. Hennessy, National Research Council.

used in scientific research, practicing human factors specialists rarely have the luxury of using properly counterbalanced experimental designs, with a range of levels of factors and the precise control of unmanipulated variables. This is not to minimize the importance of experimental methods which are used whenever possible and have provided much of the basic data in human factors handbooks. However, applied methods are necessary both as suplements to experimental methods, e.g., for problem analysis and structuring, and as substitutes when the pressures and constraints of the engineering design environment preclude experimental investigations.

Most practical work in human factors is done under conditions that involve the incomplete specification of system functions, complex combinations of conditions that cannot be separated or controlled, restricted sets of alternatives, limited time and opportunities for investigation, and pressure to produce definitive results quickly. From necessity, human factors specialists have evolved an armamentarium of applied methods that are appropriate to these conditions and that are unfamiliar to most academic researchers. These applied methods are formal means for acquiring or organizing information about human factors characteristics that arise in the context of system design, development, and evaluation.

Applied methods are diverse, reflecting the many purposes for which human factors information is used. Some of them come from psychology, for example, questionnaires and techniques for acquiring, summarizing, and analyzing data. Some have been borrowed, with or without modification, from other fields, such as industrial engineering and time and motion engineering. For example, analytic methods draw heavily on the engineering practice of systems analysis, which identifies inputs, outputs, the functions performed, the range of values that variables may assume, process flow, the sequence of events, and the timing of the interrelations of system components. Other methods, such as the critical incident technique and link analysis, appear to have been created by human factors specialists to meet their needs in solving particular problems.

Whatever their origins, applied methods have been developed as tools to help answer questions when there are constraints of time, dollars, and freedom of action and when experimental methods are not suitable to answer the questions that arise in system development. Although it is characteristic of applied methods that they make it

3.1 General Requirements
    3.1.1 Scope and Nature of Work
- Analysis
- Design/Development
- Test and Evaluation

    3.1.2 Human Engineering Program Plan and Other Data
        3.1.2.1 Human Engineering Program Plan
        3.1.2.2 Changes to the Human Engineering Program Plan
        3.1.2.3 Other Data
    3.1.3 Non Duplication (of Effort)

3.2 Detail Requirements
    3.2.1 Analysis
        3.2.1.1 Defining and Allocating System Functions
            3.2.1.1.1 Information Flow and Processing Analysis
            3.2.1.1.2 Estimates of Potential Operator/Maintainer Processing Capabilities
            3.2.1.1.3 Allocation of Functions
        3.2.1.2 Equipment Identification
        3.2.1.3 Analysis of Tasks
            3.2.1.3.1 Gross Analysis of Tasks
1. Determine System Performance Can Be Provided by Proposed Personnel-Equipment Capabilities
2. Assure Human Performance Requirements Do Not Exceed Human Capabilities
3. Input Data for
   - Preliminary Manning Levels
   - Equipment Procedures
   - Skill/Training Requirements
   - Communication Requirements
4. Critical Human Performance
5. Possible Unsafe Practice
6. Promising Improvements in Operating Efficiency

            3.2.1.3.2 Analysis of Critical Tasks
1. Identifying
   - Information Required by Man, Including Task Initiation Cues
   - Information Available to Man
   - Evaluation Process
   - Decision Reached After Evaluation
   - Action Taken
   - Body Movements Required by Action
   - Workspace Envelope Required by Action
   - Workspace Available
   - Location/Condition of Work Environment
   - Frequency/Tolerances for Action
   - Time Base
   - Feedback on Action Adequacy
   - Tools and Equipment Required
   - Number of Personnel Required and Specialties/Experience
   - Job Aids/References Required
   - Special Hazards Involved
   - Operation Interaction Where More Than One Crewman is Involved
   - Operational Limits of Man (Performance)
   - Operational Limits of Machine (State-of-the-Art)

FIGURE 7-1 Outline of Human Factors Requirements in the Development of Military Systems

    2. Covering All Affected Mission/Phases, Including Degraded Modes of Operation
  3.2.1.3.3 Loading Analysis
    1. Individual Crew Member Workload Analysis Compared with Performance Criteria
    2. Crew Workload Analysis Compared with Performance Criteria
  3.2.1.4 Preliminary System and Subsystem Design
 3.2.2 Human Engineering Studies, Experiments and Laboratory Tests
  3.2.2.1 Studies, Experiments and Laboratory Tests
   3.2.2.1.1 Mockups and Models
   3.2.2.1.2 Dynamic Simulation
  3.2.2.2 Equipment Detail Design Drawings
  3.2.2.3 Work Environment, Crew Stations and Facilities Design
   o Atmospheric Conditions
   o Weather and Climate
   o Range of Accelerative Forces
   o Acoustic Noise, Vibration and Impact Forces
   o Provision for Human Performance During Weightlessness
   o Provision for Minimizing Disorientation
   o Space for Crew, Activity and Equipment
   o Physical, Visual and Auditory Links for All Man-Equipment Interfaces
   o Safe, Efficient Walkways, Stairways, Platforms, Inclines
   o Provision to Minimize Psychophysiological Stresses
   o Provision to Minimize Fatigue--Physical, Emotional, Work-Rest Cycle
   o Protection from Hazards--Chemical, Biological, Toxicological, Radiological, Electrical, Electromagnetic
   o Optimum Illumination Per Visual Tasks
   o Sustenance, Storage and Sanitation
   o Crew Safety Protection Relative to Mission Phase and Control-Display Tasks
  3.2.2.4 Human Engineering in Performance and Design Specifications
 3.2.3 Equipment Procedure Development
 3.2.4 Human Engineering Test and Evaluation
  3.2.4.1 Planning
  3.2.4.2 Implementation (Include As Applicable)
   o Simulation or Actual Conduct of Mission/Work Cycle
   o Human Participation Critical to Speed, Accuracy, Reliability, Cost
   o Representative Sample of Non Critical Scheduled/Unscheduled Maintenance Tasks
   o Proposed Job Aids
   o Use of Representative User Personnel, Clothing and Equipment
   o Task Performance Data Collection
   o Task Performance Discrepancies--Required vs. Obtained
   o Criteria for Acceptable Performance
  3.2.4.3 Failure Analysis (Human Error Factors)
 3.2.5 Cognizance and Coordination (Interdisciplinary Integration)
3.3 Data Requirements Per Contract Data List
3.4 Data Availability to Procuring Activity
3.5 Drawing Approval by HFE for Man-Machine Interface

Source: Adapted from Parks and Springer (1976).

Accident studies	Activity analyses
Attitude studies	Cost-benefit analysis
Critical incident studies	Decision analysis
Delphi techniques	Failure mode analysis
Fault tree analysis	Flow analysis
Functional analysis	Job analysis
Lapse time photography	Link analysis
Near-accident studies	Network flow analysis
Operational sequence analysis	Questionnaires
Requirements analysis	Task analysis

FIGURE 7-2 Applied Method Names Appearing in Keyword Lists of Articles in <u>Human Factors</u> Between 1976-1981

possible to acquire and produce data and information only to the degree of resolution and reliability sufficient for a particular purpose, these methods are systematic and objective procedures. That is, the procedures are repeatable and input and output data are operationally defined.

The importance of applied methods in human factors work is clear from the number of technical reports and journal articles that discuss one or more applied methods. Two recent reports (Williges and Topmiller, 1980; Geer, 1981) list human factors procedures necessary for Air Force system analysis, design, and evaluation; the latter report gives brief descriptions and critiques of approximately 48 human engineering procedures, the majority of which are applied methods. Figure 7-2 lists applied methods that appeared in keyword lists of articles published between 1976 and 1981 in <u>Human Factors</u>, the journal of the Human Factors Society.

Despite this wide variety of applied methods, there is general agreement among human factors specialists that we need to improve existing methods and develop new ones (Topmiller, 1981; Meister, 1982). Advances in technology, particularly in the speed, power, and memory of computers, have generated concern recently with the human factors elements of computer software. At the same time, the explosive growth of computer use, with resultant increases in the complexity and integration of system components, the automation of functions, and the use of artificial intelligence, all have profound methodological implications for the analysis and description of the role of humans and computers in such systems.

Applied methods have never previously been treated as a single topic deserving attention in its own right.* Consequently, information has never been gathered on the number and varieties of applied methods available and the frequency and adequacy with which they are used. The workshop held by the Committee on Human Factors, on which the discussion in this chapter is based, was an attempt by committee members and a group of acknowledged experts in applied methods to identify problems and needs with respect to applied methods. Even in the absence of data on the variety and frequency of use of applied methods, we have been able to identify several major problems and to recommend solutions, which may make substantial improvements in practice possible. Three major problems are discussed: (1) the lack of adequate documentation; (2) the limited opportunities available to learn applied methods, either in colleges and universities offering human factors courses or as part of the continuing education of human factors specialists; and (3) the lack of research to improve existing methods and to develop new methods that will provide the data and information needed in current and future practical human factors work.

DOCUMENTATION OF APPLIED METHODS

The practical work of human factors specialists, unlike scientific research, does not result in an orderly progression and an orderly accumulation of knowledge. Human factors projects (i.e., participation in the design of systems) and the solution of special problems come and go in great variety. Typically work is performed, reported, and forgotten as new systems and problems develop. Codified, archival repositories of practical work--i.e., review books and articles that summarize the knowledge and procedures used in human factors applications to some point in time--are rare. As a result the historical memory of human factors methods resides largely in the heads and in the report files of practitioners. By contrast, in the literature on scientific research, the

---

*This situation contrasts with experimental methods, for which there are many textbooks and source books for readers at all levels of sophistication.

methods used by investigators are maintained and disseminated in the curricula of university departments and preserved on library bookshelves.

As an important first step toward improving knowledge about and use of applied methods, we therefore recommend that one or more projects be initiated to compile and review the available information on applied methodologies used in human factors and related fields, such as industrial and organizational psychology, personnel selection, and instructional psychology. The object of the review would be to determine what methods have been used, how they have been used, where they are used, and what their advantages and disadvantages are. The project should also include a critical analysis of the methods. Other purposes of the review would be to structure or codify the methods and to document them for subsequent educational and research purposes.

It would also be extremely valuable to practitioners, educators, and researchers in human factors to have a compendium that codifies and provides standard or generic descriptions of applied methods that are used in practical human factors work. Development of such a compendium would require a great deal of judicious and careful effort. One of the primary difficulties would be to decide which methods are viable, valid, and useful. Because such a compendium would necessarily be an implicit endorsement of the methods described, we recommend that eight criteria be used in the selection process. Methods that meet the criteria listed below could be regarded as having sufficient stature to be of value in a variety of human factors applications:

Importance--Does the method produce needed information?
Cost--Is the method efficient in terms of effort and time?
Utility--Can procedures for using the method be easily interpreted and implemented?
Available Input Parameters--Can the necessary data be collected in a direct, objective, and reliable way?
Usable Output--Does the method produce results that are interpretable and useful for decision making?
Validity/Verification--Can or has the method been found to produce the information it is supposed to?

Theoretical Foundation--Is the method supported by
 accepted behavioral or measurement principles?
Robustness--Can the method be applied to a variety of
 problems or in different contexts?

These criteria imply that the approach to documenting standard definitions of applied methods should be conservative. That is, only those methods for which there is evidence of practicality and validity should be selected for inclusion in a compendium. Methods used in workload assessment provide an example of the importance of using these criteria. Measurement of workload is a current topic of intense research interest; consequently a large number of theories, approaches, and positions have been put forward. Since most of the recent work has not been validated through practical application, it would be inappropriate to describe them as standard, accepted methods. Older methods exist for assessing imposed workload that, while perhaps wanting in certain respects, have been proven through repeated use to be practical, reliable, and valid (Parks and Springer, 1976) and are likely to meet our criteria. Nevertheless, there will be hard choices to make in deciding what constitutes an accepted, standard form of a method.

Multiple variations of a method should probably not be included. A compendium that includes only a set of core methods that meet the criteria would be of great value for both practical work on system development and as a foundation for the education of human factors students at colleges and universities. Attempting comprehensive coverage of all variations of methods would unnecessarily complicate the task of documentation and delay the compilation, causing confusion and consequently inhibiting its acceptance. A single, solid definition of each particular method would be most useful, since by its nature an applied method undergoes some variation in each instance of its use because of the requirements and constraints of a particular project. In the meantime, additional documentation and research to extend or refine the standard methods can be carried out.

In the course of compiling a reasonably comprehensive list of the most generally known applied methods (see Figure 3), it became apparent that the methodologies could be grouped into five categories according to their purpose. Five categories of applied methodologies seem appropriate: analysis, identification of needs, data collection, prediction, and evaluation. Each methodology appears only under one heading, although several of them are appropriate to more than one category.

The organization of Figure 7-3 is probably a useful guide to the scope of work involved in documenting applied methods. The categories reflect a sequence of methods used, from the early concept definition of a system to its evaluation. There is also a rough correlation between the difficulty and detail involved in particular methods and the stage of application in the process of system development.

Documentation of applied methods necessarily requires review of the technical literature to extract descriptions of applied methods. To expect a single or a small group of experts to adequately review and document the entire range of applied methods would be impractical; a more feasible approach would be to subdivide the work according to the five categories of purpose. The individual tasks would thereby be more tractable and make better use of the skills of individuals whose knowledge and expertise is likely to be confined to a single category rather than the full range of methods. This approach would also allow the work on each subset of methods to be performed concurrently. Whatever the approach taken, producing a compendium of standard, usable descriptions of proven applied methods would be an extremely valuable contribution to the field of human factors and consequently to the future development of human-machine systems.

SURVEY OF HUMAN FACTORS SPECIALISTS ON APPLIED METHODS

Because of the dearth of information on the variety and use of applied methods in human factors work we recommend a survey of human factors practitioners concerned with the acquisition, design, development, and evaluation or modification of equipment and systems. Such a survey would determine the importance and frequency of use of existing applied methods in their work; the kind of information most needed in human factors applications for which existing applied methodologies are inadequate or nonexistent; and the methods for which descriptions and guidance for use are most needed.

The survey would provide the necessary information on which to base documentation, education, and research efforts. Review, codification, standardization, and documentation of existing methods should proceed

ANALYSIS

System Analysis
Function/Task Analysis
Information Analysis
Scenario Analysis
Workload Analysis
Time-Line Analysis
Operational Sequence Analysis
Failure Mode Analysis
Fault Tree Analysis
Link Analysis
Function Allocation
Anthropometric Analysis
Decision Analysis
Display Evaluation Index

IDENTIFICATION OF NEEDS

Critical Incident Technique
Surveys/Questionnaires
Accident Investigation
Interviews/Group Techniques
Definition of User Population

DATA COLLECTION

Activity Analysis
Time Lapse Photography
Real Time Film/Video Recording
Direct Observation
Physiological Recording
Quantitative Performance
  Recording and Analysis

PREDICTION

The Human Error Rate Procedure
  (THERP)
Data Store
Human Operator Simulator (HOS)
Control Theory
Accuracy Theory
Predetermined Time Analysis
Readability Indices

EVALUATION

Test Plan Evaluation
Simulation
Mock-Ups
Walk Throughs
Check Lists
Ratings

FIGURE 7-3 Generally Known Applied Methods Categorized by Purpose

according to the priorities of importance and frequency of use derived from the survey. Information from the survey would be useful in shaping human factors curricula in colleges and universities so that students can be trained in applied methods that they will subsequently need on the job. The continuing education needs of human factors specialists could also be met by means of tutorials and symposia on the applied methods for which there is the greatest need for information. Finally, the results of the survey would provide a sound basis for basic research efforts to extend or improve existing methods or develop new methods to meet these needs.

Construction of the survey instrument itself would require a review of the technical literature for descriptions and definitions of applied methods, which the survey recipients would be expected to rate. The literature review would also provide additional data, complementary to the anticipated survey, on the variety and frequency of use of applied methods reflected in the technical literature. A product of this review would be a relatively comprehensive bibliography of technical reports and journal articles that discuss applied methods in more than a cursory fashion; this bibliographic information would be extremely valuable for subsequent efforts on the codification and documentation of existing methods and the initiation of research efforts to extend these methods or develop new ones.

EDUCATION IN APPLIED METHODS

Education in Colleges and Universities

The absence of codified information and the lack of easy access to source reports inhibits instruction in applied methods at colleges and universities that offer degree programs or courses in the field of human factors. General human factors textbooks give at best only a cursory overview of a few applied methods and present case study examples that highlight the substantive issues and results rather than the methods. There are no texts suitable either for college-level instruction or as a reference for practicing human factors specialists that adequately treat applied methods. The single exception, <u>Research Techniques in Human Engineering</u> (Chapanis, 1959), discusses only a limited set of methods. For the most part, instructors must rely on their own experience and the descriptions of applied methods gleaned from the technical literature to develop course material. They have no current and comprehensive reference works to develop a balanced and thorough course in applied methods.

Human factors work is diverse and is performed in many settings--i.e., military research and development centers, other government facilities, and commercial organizations. Ideally, instruction in applied methods would emphasize the methods of most use in real-life settings. Without data on the variety and frequency of use it is difficult to decide which applied methods should be taught in human factors courses at the undergraduate and graduate levels. Clearly the development of a compendium of applied methods, as recommended in the previous section, would be of substantial benefit for formal educational purposes. Until such a compendium exists and survey data is compiled on the variety, frequency of use, and capabilities of applied methods, no meaningful recommendations can be made to improve education in applied methods in colleges and universities.

Continuing Education in Applied Methods

Of equal concern is the lack of suitable continuing education courses in applied methods for practicing human factors specialists. The problem of inadequate methodological preparation in formal education extends to the work setting. At present it appears that many presumably well-trained human factors specialists work without adequate knowledge of applied methods, and what knowledge they do have about these methods is acquired on the job.

Currently employed human factors specialists could benefit greatly from continuing education in applied methods specifically related to their current work. Development at colleges and universities of educational programs in applied methods that provide a thorough treatment of a range of applied methods would require a substantial amount of planning and course design work. Undoubtedly the broad inception of these programs, and the realization of their eventual benefits in practice, will be some time in coming. Unlike formal education in applied methods, however, the development of courses for continuing education could be done more easily and produce more immediate positive effects. Human factors professionals are likely to be more easily educated because of their general knowledge of human factors techniques and the likelihood that they have at least a working familiarity with some applied methods. Because of their previous education and experience, continuing education courses for them can be much more practical, with less emphasis on theoretical foundations. Based on the membership of the Human Factors Society, which numbers nearly 3,000, a reasonable estimate of the actual number of practicing human factors specialists in this country who could benefit from continuing education in applied methods is between 5,000 and 10,000.

Fostering and promoting continuing education by means of tutorials on applied methods is one of the most important and immediate ways to improve the field of human factors. Moreover, this kind of activity could most easily be initiated by military and other federal agencies charged with advancing scientific and engineering knowledge and practice. These tutorials could directly benefit human factors specialists employed by the government as well as those employed by civilian organizations that develop equipment and systems for the government. It is therefore recommended that initial tutorials on applied methods be developed and conducted under the sponsorship of one or more government agencies. While we suggest methods to be discussed in the tutorial below, it would be more prudent to base the choice on a needs analysis of the data derived from the survey recommended above.

Such a tutorial could serve several purposes besides the obvious one of improving the professional competence of human factors specialists. First, the materials generated for the tutorial would contribute to the development of standard definitions and documentation of applied methods, since the course materials would have to describe the subject methods with sufficient care and detail to allow human factors specialists to use them easily and properly. Second, the tutorials would be a means for validating a prior needs analysis of which applied methods are considered most important to human factors practitioners. Attendance at the tutorials would also help answer a more fundamental question: Is there genuine interest in learning about applied methods? Third, the initial tutorial would serve as a test to evaluate instructional methods and course structures for training in the use of applied methods.

It is suggested that the initial tutorial should consist of three parts: (1) an introductory review of the applied methodologies within each of the five categories listed in Figure 7-3; (2) a comparison of techniques within each category and a discussion of how to select the appropriate method for a particular application; and (3) detailed instruction and practical work on a few selected methods. We suggest five particular methodologies as subjects for the initial tutorial:

> Task analysis;
> Time line analysis;
> Activities analysis;
> Simulation; and
> Information Analysis.

Because these methods as well as others are either poorly or inconsistently defined, brief definitions of the five methods recommended for the first tutorial are given in Appendix A. It would not be practical to cover more than five methodologies at the initial tutorial; five may even be too many.

There are a number of other specific concerns relevant to the form and development of a tutorial on applied methods. Experience has shown tutorials to be only the first step in learning to use a particular technique properly. Generally, an individual needs several days of supervised application to become competent in using a particular method. Therefore, the tutorial should not be simply a symposium but rather should be a workshop in which the attendees could gain hands-on experience. A by-product of the initial tutorial would be the development and testing of the structure and effectiveness of the initial instructional methods.

A tutorial on applied methods would probably require 10 to 40 hours of planning and preparing for each hour of instructional time. Since the tutorial should include practical workshop exercises in addition to lecture, a good part of the effort of preparation would have to be devoted to development of materials. It is likely that the practicum would require one or more assistants in addition to the instructor.

An individual or small group should be selected to develop a master plan for the tutorial workshop. The primary goal would be to choose the methods to be taught in the tutorial. This determination should be based largely on the needs analysis of the data gathered from the methods survey of human factors practitioners recommended above. The individual or group should also address such issues as the number of days the tutorial should run, whether it should be conducted independently or in association with a national meeting, the estimated costs, and the selection of instructors.

The most obvious audience for the first tutorial are human factors practitioners, although the needs of other groups of professionals that could benefit from learning about applied methods, such as engineers, managers, students, and university teachers, should be considered at some point. Engineers are an important audience since they are likely to need to use applied methods in the course of system design and development and they are not likely to know where to seek information on methodologies. Managers are important because of their influential role in equipment and system development. Due to their position of authority, managers are able to influence practices of their employees. College and university teachers are a relevant audience, since what they learn would be passed on to their students. And students, especially students in engineering and human factors, are a particularly important potential audience because of their receptivity to new techniques and the apparent lack of adequate education in applied methods in colleges and universities.

The tutorial format appropriate for human factors professionals may not be suitable for these other groups. If the first tutorial proves to be beneficial to human factors specialists, it would be worthwhile to design others tailored to the backgrounds and needs of these other groups. We recommend that tutorials for these other groups be developed first for engineers and subsequently for the remaining groups.

For all audiences the tutorials should be repeated at several times and locations both to make the experience available to all who are interested and to recover the initial development costs.

RESEARCH ON APPLIED METHODS

Each applied method was originated to fill some particular need for information to support system design, evaluation, or problem analysis. Through a succession of repeated, successful use in different contexts, methods have evolved and have become known and accepted as tools of the trade in human factors work. Because they were developed as a means to some practical end and so vary in form depending on the situations in which they are used, there has never been very much concern about their refinement or extension. That is, an applied method has rarely been regarded as an important topic worthy of research investigation in its own right, independent of a particular use. This lack of status is partly reflected and partly caused by the absence of standard documentation of applied methods. In addition, the people who use applied methods are practitioners and, in some sense, generalists in human factors rather than specialists in methodology. There is no body of experts who devote their careers to the study and development of applied methods rather than their actual use, as there is for experimental design and statistical analysis.

Applied methods, however, are the principal means by which human factors work is accomplished. In light of their contibution to systems work, applied methods are a sufficently important topic to deserve research attention. Advances should not depend solely on incidental efforts made by human factors specialists in the course of their work. Basic research specifically devoted to the validation, refinement, and extension of existing methods and to the development of new methods is essential.

Improvement and Extension of Existing Applied Methods

As previously discussed, fundamental problems are the lack of documented definitions and descriptions of existing applied methods and the lack of knowledge about what information is needed in human factors work. Documentation and survey work is necessary to provide baseline descriptions and to help identify the particular problems and shortcomings of existing methods.

Without this information it is difficult to specify what research on which particular methods would have the greatest value in terms of its contribution to the improvement of human factors work. Nonetheless, we propose some existing methods as subjects deserving research attention because from our experience it is apparent that these methods are widely used, critical to system design and development work, and could be substantially improved: workload analysis; function allocation; task analysis; survey techniques; and protocol analysis.

Workload analysis is already the subject of many ongoing research programs; however, it is important enough to merit expanded support for research on workload assessment methods. While the five methods named above are, in our opinion, most deserving of research attention, the order of presentation should not be construed as indicating priorities among them. There is insufficient knowledge about the needs of the human factors community to assign priorities.

Development of New Applied Methods

In discussing current and future problems and trends in human factors applications to system development, Meister (1980, 1982) has identified those informational requirements of human factors specialists that imply needs for the development of new applied methods. On the basis of these suggestions, we make general recommendations for research leading to the development of five new applied methods:

1. Methods for interpreting or extrapolating task/system requirements into personnel requirements;
2. Performance measurement methods that express measures in terms relative to base rates for particular system characteristics and/or demands;
3. Training technology methods for translating task/abilities requirements into training programs;
4. System evaluation methods--static, dynamic, and comparative; and
5. Methods for describing and evaluating task or system impact on affective responses of personnel.

SUMMARY

There is a serious disparity between the importance of applied methodologies for human factors work, particularly systems and equipment design, and the efforts being made to document and codify them in a standard manner; to educate behavioral science and engineering students in their use in colleges and universities; to provide continuing education in applied methods to working human factors specialists; and to engage in research to improve existing applied methodologies and develop new ones. It is of great importance to document what is currently known about applied methods. Increasing the accessibility of information on existing methods would be more valuable than developing new methods. What follows is a summary of our recommendations with respect to applied methods.

* Existing methodologies should be assessed and documented in a codified compendium that provides standard descriptions of the most useful applied methods. This compendium would serve both as a comprehensive and readily available source for learning about and as a basis for determining specific research needs.
* Human factors practitioners should be surveyed to determine the importance and frequency of use of existing applied methods in their work; the kinds of information most needed in human factors applications for which existing applied methods are inadequate or nonexistent; and methods for which they require descriptions and guidance for use.
* Tutorials on applied methods should be developed to meet the continuing educational needs of human factors specialists. Methods recommended for the initial tutorial are: task analysis; time line analysis; activities analysis; simulation; and information analysis.
* Basic research should be performed to improve and extend existing applied methods. Methods in need of research include: workload analysis; function allocation; task analysis; survey techniques; and protocol analysis.
* Basic research is also required to develop new methods that can provide the information needed by human factors specialists to do their work. New methods needed include: (1) methods for interpreting or extrapolating task/system requirements into personnel selection requirements; (2) performance measurement methods that express measures in terms relative to base rates for particular system characteristics and/or demands; (3) training technology methods for translating task/abilities requirements into training programs; (4) system evaluation methods--static, dynamic, and comparative; and (5) methods for describing and evaluating task or system impact on affective responses of personnel.

REFERENCES

Chapanis, A.
    1959   <u>Research Techniques in Human Engineering</u>. Baltimore, Md.: Johns Hopkins University Press.

Geer, C. W.
    1981   <u>Human Engineering Procedures Guide</u>. Report AFAMRL-TR-81-35. Wright-Patterson Air Force Base, Ohio: Air Force Aerospace Medical Research Laboratory.

Meister, D.
1980   Human Factors for the Future--Trends and
        Speculations. In <u>Proceedings of Symposium on
        Human Factors in Systems Development:
        Experience and Trends</u>. Karlstadt, Sweden:
        National Defense Research Institute.

Meister, D.
1982   The role of human factors in system
        development. <u>Applied Ergonomics</u> 13:119-124.

Parks, D. L., and Springer, W. E.
1976   <u>Human Factors Engineering Analytic Process
        Definition and Criterion Development for CAFES</u>
        (Computer Aided Function-Allocation Evaluation
        System). Warminster, Pa.: Naval Air
        Development Center.

Topmiller, D. A.
1981   Methods: past approaches, current trends and
        future requirements. In M. J. Moraal and K.
        F. Kraiss, eds., <u>Manned System Design</u>. New
        York: Plenum Press.

Williges, R. C., and Topmiller, D. A.
1980   <u>Task III: Technology Assessment of Human
        Factors Engineering in the Air Force</u>.
        Wright-Patterson Air Force Base, Ohio: Air
        Force Systems Command.

APPENDIX

SHORT DEFINITIONS OF APPLIED METHODS RECOMMENDED AS SUBJECTS FOR TUTORIAL

Task Analysis

Task analysis is the process of analyzing functional requirements of a system to ascertain and describe the tasks that people must perform. Task analysis has two major aspects: The first specifies and describes the tasks; the second and more important analyzes the specified tasks to determine the number of people needed, the skills and knowledge they should have, and the training necessary. Results of task analysis are used in the development of operating procedures and technical manuals and the determination of critical equipment characteristics and task demands imposed on people. The analytic method involves decomposition of task content into their constituent elements, such as stimulus input, required response, equipment output, and feedback information.

Simulation

Simulation is used (1) to allow users to experience, in advance of its operation, portions of a system that are more complex, more dangerous, or more expensive than an experiment could allow for or (2) to predict performance of systems that do not exist. Simulation is a human factors methodology only when it is combined with one of the observational or measurement methodologies. And to extrapolate the observations or measurements to the real world requires a determination of the extent to which things that affect the observations of interest are realistically portrayed in the simulation. How to make this determination (cost/transfer function, part versus whole task simulation, which things to simulate) is the key part of the technology that is still largely unresolved. In the absence of other effective means of predicting the behavioral consequences of system design, simulation is crucial.

Time Line Analysis

Time line analysis organizes a detailed task list for the operational scenario and procedures into serial order and plots the times of individual tasks in sequence against a time base. It portrays sequential, parallel, repeated, and/or intermittent tasks according to what is done. The resulting accumulation of tasks and total performance time can be used to appraise:

1. The validity of the operations to be performed in contributing to system objectives;
2. The feasibility of performing required tasks within the required time;
3. Antecedent hardware and operations conditions to ensure that the requirements of each task element are met;
4. The compatibility of demands on the operator, ensuring that antecedent tasks are identified and performed, required skills and performances are feasible and practical, and difficult, complex, or conflicting demands are avoided; and

5. Workload demands, by comparing time requirements to complete a task series to the time available for completion within the constraints of a given system.

Information Analysis

Information analysis identifies information and its flow through a system, usually as perceived from a user's viewpoint. For example, the flow of information necessary for the operation of an office differs from the flow of documents through that office. Certain system actions occur to the information received, which in turn becomes inputs to subsequent actions. Information analyses enable human factors specialists to assess and design the information requirements of the user interfaces.

Activity Analysis

In many situations involving field environments, simulations, or mock-ups, it is desirable and useful to catalog the distribution and/or sequential dependencies of workers' activities. In activity analysis an observer periodically or aperiodically samples the work being performed and classifies the results into a set of categories. The data may be obtained from direct observation or from video or film recording. Individual samples are then aggregated into activity frequency tables or graphs or state transition diagrams. These analyses are especially useful for documenting the way in which task requirements change with alternative system designs or environments or for estimates of relative cost effectiveness, manning requirements, or simply for understanding how individuals or groups spend their time.

Unclassified
SECURITY CLASSIFICATION OF THIS PAGE (When Data Entered)

REPORT DOCUMENTATION PAGE

READ INSTRUCTIONS
BEFORE COMPLETING FORM

1. REPORT NUMBER	2. GOVT ACCESSION NO.	3. RECIPIENT'S CATALOG NUMBER

4. TITLE (and Subtitle)	5. TYPE OF REPORT & PERIOD COVERED
Research Needs for Human Factors	Technical
	6. PERFORMING ORG. REPORT NUMBER

7. AUTHOR(s)	8. CONTRACT OR GRANT NUMBER(s)
Committee on Human Factors	N00014-81-C-0017

9. PERFORMING ORGANIZATION NAME AND ADDRESS	10. PROGRAM ELEMENT, PROJECT, TASK AREA & WORK UNIT NUMBERS
National Research Council 2101 Constitution Avenue, N.W. Washington, D.C. 20418	Work Unit No. NR196-167

11. CONTROLLING OFFICE NAME AND ADDRESS	12. REPORT DATE
Engineering Psychology Programs Office of Naval Research Arlington, VA 22217	January 19, 1983
	13. NUMBER OF PAGES

14. MONITORING AGENCY NAME & ADDRESS(if different from Controlling Office)	15. SECURITY CLASS. (of this report)
	Unclassified
	15a. DECLASSIFICATION/DOWNGRADING SCHEDULE

16. DISTRIBUTION STATEMENT (of this Report)

Approved for Public Release; Distribution Unlimited

17. DISTRIBUTION STATEMENT (of the abstract entered in Block 20, if different from Report)

18. SUPPLEMENTARY NOTES

19. KEY WORDS (Continue on reverse side if necessary and identify by block number)

Human Factors Research
Human Engineering Research
Engineering Psychology Research
Human Decision Making
Expert Judgment
Human Computer Interaction
Supervisory Control Systems
Population Group Differences
Human Factors Methodology

20. ABSTRACT (Continue on reverse side if necessary and identify by block number)

This report describes basic research needed to improve the scientific basis of applied human factors work. Six topical areas are covered; 1) human decision making; 2) eliciting information from experts; 3) user-computer interaction; 4) supervisory control systems; 5) population group differences; and 6) applied methods.

DD FORM 1473   EDITION OF 1 NOV 65 IS OBSOLETE
S N 0102-LF-014-6601

Unclassified
SECURITY CLASSIFICATION OF THIS PAGE (When Data Entered)